THE RULE BREAKER

We only have two choices...

MS. K

Cover Design by Brian Buchholtz and Laurie Griffin
Interior Design by Scottie A.B.

Funded and produced by BookRally:

www.bookrally.com

ISBN: 978-1-946503-11-4

Printed in the United States.

Dedication

This story is dedicated to the potential of humanity, to the common ground we must stand on, and to the courage we need right now to unite and have faith in the source. Our future is what we decide it to be, and when we ignite our limitless powers, that future looks brighter than ever.

This story exists to demonstrate the super-human abilities that we all possess so that we can utilize our inherent gifts and co-create a world where we all thrive. The purpose is to encourage people to tap into their intrinsic abilities, understand their healing powers, and pursue their individual path toward higher consciousness.

The intention of this book is to enliven our collective heart by empowering people to reach their potential and master a way of thinking that inflames their soul. We are a magnificent species and our potential is limitless. This book was created to demonstrate the necessity of unnerving faith so that humanity can intentionally illuminate this world more than ever before. This book is dedicated to our freedom!

Acknowledgments

From the bottom of my heart, thank you to everyone who helped guide me during this painful journey and contributed to my growth. Special thanks to the intuitive guides who came blasting into my life and coached me through this.

There is limitless gratitude for my teachers, mentors, healers, spirit guides and soul mates. I'm so blessed and I love you! And to GG—Merry Christmas—"you my go to"!

To my spiritual tribe, thank you for the healing, unconditional love and inspiration—you saved my life—the world needs more warriors like you! I'm so grateful I found you!

To my family, friends and anyone whom I hurt, I am sorry beyond words! Thank you for your forgiveness—let's heal and heal the world! I love you so much!

Lastly, thank you to everyone who tried to stop me—you were the fuel that got me here! I love you and I'm stronger because of you!

Table of Contents

Introduction

For anyone in search of answers, purpose and deeper connection to this earth, please open your mind and take this ride. For those who enjoy adventure, risk taking and raw madness, please buckle up. And for those who love the drama, you're in the right spot!

This book is for those who want to break free from societal and inner restraints so that they can view the world from an empowering vantage point. This story will help you blow past your limitations of what is possible and get excited about the magic that is all around us.

If you are in need of clarity, an escape from conditioned thinking and a blast of inspiration, then this story is that beam of hope. This journey is for those who want to see change in our world and need direction. This story is for those who have the courage to believe in the power of our Universe. This book is for you if you're reading this!

There will be specific manifesting techniques and tips summarized at the end of the book, as well as a list of resources and where to follow me, to help you manifest faster and with more ease. It's time for you to master your mind, your life and the Law of Attraction!

1

GROUNDED

I don't know how I ended up on the floor—the ability to care had vanished. With the sound of his last door slam still echoing in my ears, my legs had hopelessly flopped beneath me, and I was just done. Done making the same mistakes. Done playing it safe. Done feeling trapped. Just done. Something had to change—and fast. *How is this my life?*

I had just been walking down the hall and was now observing my melted self from an inexplicably detached vantage point. Tears of vulnerability and pain streamed down my face as I begged for guidance. *I surrender. I promise I won't ever lose myself in a relationship again. I'm sorry. Please help me understand, and reach, my purpose.*

If there had been a white flag next to me, I would have waved it enthusiastically. My playful spirit and positive nature were missed—they were lost in a whirlwind of colliding emotions among a screaming match of thoughts. The chaotic search for them had begun.

Despite my weakened body and spinning mind, I was also aware of a massive wave of relief sweeping through my soul. It was over, and I had finally been released from the imprisonment of my former relationship. I was free.

◊

The last two months had been torturous, as we continued living together after the breakup while he reluctantly looked for an apartment. He thought he could talk me out of it, but the nightmare breakup was in forward motion only.

I had wanted out for so long but never had the courage to commit to the irreversible finality. The fear had always bullied me out of it. It was now time to take responsibility for the reality I had created. Resisting the urge to self-scold was in vain. *Why didn't I get out sooner?*

My mind scrambled to process the myriad of mistakes made. I had ignored all the red flags, made too many sacrifices, put his needs before mine, had unrealistic expectations, romanticized everything, quieted my instincts, believed that I could change him, let my emotions get the best of me, made up excuses for him, and passively witnessed the progressive loss of my true self. Clarity and regrets raced each other to the surface.

To prevent this from happening again, a monumental transformation was necessary. It was time to completely rewire my inner self and redesign my reality. Reconnecting with my core required new depths of self-exploration. *Wow, I can do anything I want to now—it's a fresh start. What do I want my life to look like? How do I make this happen?*

A conscious decision was made to forgive myself, forgive him, and then learn from it, release it, and move on. There was no point in overanalyzing or harboring bad feelings. It just didn't work out. I *had* to let it all go, so I did.

Once the ache of separating started to subside, my newfound independence became intoxicating. I couldn't help but feel gratitude for my now single status—the possibilities for personal development and adventure were beyond my comprehension.

Every passing moment of this new awareness was like soaking in a potent bath of empowerment and freedom. The nostalgic aroma that was filling my home soothed me as the pain began to wash away in a therapeutic cleanse.

A flood of wisdom forcefully began surging through me as it carried me into a state of awe. There was so much to take in. As I went through this process, sensations of peace, energy, and truth started to course through me, encapsulating every cell in my body. Something primal had awakened, and my soul was on fire. *What is this? What's happening to me? Why does it feel so familiar?*

Feeling invigorated, I quickly started writing down all of the most profound thoughts and philosophies that were pouring into my mind. It was as though someone had finally turned on the lights. I couldn't figure out why they had been off in the first place. Either way, the fog had lifted. My new residence was a puzzlingly remote and protected state of consciousness. An outside observer wasn't meant to understand; how could they?

This continued for months. My thoughts were all consuming, so outside of work I rarely left the house. It was time for unconditional love—for myself. It was time to create a new *me*.

Seclusion was necessary. It was as if the silence were whispering clues for my soul, nursing me back to health. The messages I was receiving were from a place of higher awareness and expansion—a comforting companionship that I instinctually recognized. My addictive personality had discovered new depths of self-exploration and had latched on tightly with a sense of permanency.

I began to evaluate and question everything I had done in life thus far, everything I had been told about life, and everything I wanted out of life. I saw holes in the story that society had always drilled into my mind. I wanted to learn the truth. I wanted to see the whole picture. I wanted answers. *How can I impact the world?*

At this time, I decided not to own a TV anymore—there just wasn't time. Instead, I eagerly dove into a dynamic blend of studies, reading, writing, working out, cooking, and—my truest love—dancing. If it was good for my soul, I was doing it. I had let someone dull my shine, and it was now time to come back brighter than ever.

I danced for hours each night, lost in music. Inflamed with creative energy, I painted the mental pictures of who I wanted to become and the experiences I wanted to embark on. The life I had always sensed was now an obsession to reach. My journey had started, and there was no looking back. There was momentum, despite my stillness.

Each song systematically washed away painful memories as I mentally time-warped through history, feeling connected to women from the past with each passing genre of music. Their souls were speaking to me, and I was all ears.

I imagined what their lives had been like and wondered what they would think of women in society now. *Would they be disappointed in us? Would they be proud? Would they feel that their efforts for equality are appreciated and respected? How do our struggles differ? What experiences are constant, regardless of the variable of time? Why is our collective history so grievous? Who is profiting off of our insecurities?*

I found strength in their strength as I sponged wisdom from their pain. Pondering the future of humanity, deep thoughts bombarded me. *What will life be like for our children? What about our grandchildren? What effect will all this technology have on us? What are we sacrificing for it? How do we save our planet? How do we heal?* There were limitless avenues of exploration.

It was during this time that I was able to tap into an energy source that had been suppressed for so long. It was time to take risks, to face fears, and to break away from social rules and norms. Intentions were set to morph into my potential. I vowed to the higher powers to become the best version of myself and promised to chase my dreams and fulfill my mysterious purpose.

It was at that exact moment that I had unknowingly agreed to something that entailed more than I could ever have comprehended. Had someone even vaguely told me what was about to happen, I would have laughed and said, "You're out of your mind!" I would have said, "There is no way I can do all of that!" I would have firmly proclaimed, "I can't; that's impossible—and I'm way too scared."

It was best that the complexity and incalculable vulnerability of the upcoming journey were withheld, for there was plenty of fear as it was. Had I known, I would have resisted this calling and missed out on mind-blowing experiences that changed the course of my life. I would have missed out on my story, which changed my belief system and taught me who I am and why I am here.

In the journey that ensues, there is no shortage of ups and downs, twists and turns, disasters, heartbreak, and unforeseen characters. The scenes change rapidly, so please buckle up and take this contorted ride with me.

The self-realizations, personal transformations, miracles, and magical synchronicities have left me shocked to the core. This bizarre quest for truth made my life as melodramatic as a movie—an eclectic reel of cinematic entertainment and suspense—only real.

Please try to keep an open mind, because some of it is hard to conceive, considering my comprehension of it continues to unveil. This story is not easy to share. Without personally experiencing this, it sounds far-fetched. As you'll learn, much of it is absolutely *crazy*.

It was breaking free from social conditioning, applying ancient wisdom, and learning the power of faith that opened up the doors to ... well, everything. Behind those doors were the truths that the greatest teachers throughout history were in agreement upon, and it's time to pass them along—and go one step further. It's my purpose. I've waited a long time for this and, as painful as this is, these truths need to be told.

2

TUG OF WAR

It was just a couple months later, and I couldn't believe *we* were still having the same argument. *I said absolutely not!*

"It's time to move to Chicago."

This repetitive phrase was tormenting me. *We* had been back and forth about this for months. How many times did I have to repeat myself? It was out of the question, and I was tired of being badgered about it. This was far too scary and unconventional, not to mention overwhelming and painful. How could I leave Sonoma, my beloved Sonoma? *No, I'm not moving to Chicago.*

Many people might assume that a continual debate like this would be with the person I live with or a boyfriend. I, on the other hand, was happily single and had been actively enjoying the last few months of reclaiming my life. This went deeper—much deeper.

Ironically, my persistent sidekick plays the role of a relentlessly opinionated gut. My feisty friend has always been loud and clear about what it knows, wants, and will do. It's like having two minds that both think they are right, and one adamantly refuses to compromise or give up.

We have always argued because it stubbornly demands that I do unfamiliar and challenging things, and I resist in vain. *No, I'm not moving to Chicago. I'm comfortable right where I am.*

"*It's time to move to Chicago.*"

Yeah, no thanks. This was a time of unprecedented balance and financial comfort, and I just wanted to slow down and enjoy life. Balance was something that had never been easy for a type-A personality and workaholic such as myself.

However, this knowing feeling was unshakeable. I was being assured that if I visualized what I wanted to happen, full-heartedly believed it would work out, quit my jobs, got rid of all my possessions, didn't arrange anything, packed up my car, drove to an unfamiliar city, and started my PhD, it would all work out.

Even more perplexing than that, there was a sense that this whole new life would manifest in just three days of arriving there without planning a drop of the transition. *Um, what? How is this possible? I have no idea how to do this.*

My chatty sidekick had finally gone too far. There was undeniable exhaustion from wrestling with the notion of leaving my realm of existence—my safe bubble of being—especially for absolute uncertainty. *Seriously though, how can I pull off such a drastic move by myself? Nah, I'm good; I'm not moving to Chicago.*

"*It's time to move to Chicago.*"

It was a test of faith, and I was being asked to leap. Naturally, this was hard to believe. It was a magnetic pull that could not be overpowered. No matter how hard I tried to resist, it had a hold on me. I had wanted to live there but assumed that a radical change like that would be with someone else. The idea of living in a city alone was suffocating this small-town girl.

The support system there was nonexistent, and it's not as if I had a job offer or any other reason to entice me to make such a dramatic change. This was the point where overwhelming resistance and undeniable intrigue began to butt heads. *How can I pull this off? What would happen if I did? Wait, I can't do this!*

"It's time to move to Chicago."

The floodgate on the river of excuses had clearly been lifted— and I was going under. *What if I can't find an apartment for weeks? Or what if I can't get a job for months? What if I have to use all the school money I had worked so hard to save? What if I don't get accepted into school? What if I'm lonely? What if...what if...what if? Ahh, enough of this!*

My gut was clearly voting for Chicago, Sonoma had my heart, and they were both monopolizing my mind. It was cognitive dissonance at its finest. As a hostage to my indecisiveness and defiant nature, this was an all-consuming decision.

"It's time to move to Chicago."

No one was aware of my daily torment, and I intended to keep it that way. This was a personal decision, based not on logic, outside opinions, or deductive reasoning. It was mine, and mine alone. *Yikes, what should I do? Coming back is always an option.*

Then it occurred to me: I had never regretted trying something new, regardless of the outcome, because of the indispensable personal growth. Of course there were previous situations where fear had led to excuses to not try things, leaving me wondering what could have been. Clarity barreled through my mind, confirming that congealing was not an option for my wild spirit.

Taking the unconventional road less traveled was clearly resonating. Racking up life experience and adventures while I was young and able to was certainly appealing—that's what older people had always told me to do. Challenging the "American Dream" and exploring were flirtatiously tempting. Having the courage to cut the anchors and sail away—well, that sounded divine. *Well, there it is; the scale just tipped.*

An official announcement on Facebook that I was moving quickly sealed the deal. Silly, I know, but how could I turn back now? Life is a book, and I was eager to read the next chapters, which meant that passing this test of faith was the only option. *Fine, I'll move to Chicago. I hope you have a plan, Universe, because I sure don't!*

3

ANY EXPLANATION?

It was finally game time. The reality hit as I stood in my empty apartment. The bareness of the walls was causing my eyes to blur with tears—I loved my place. *Am I doing the right thing? Is this crazy? Well, there's no turning back now. The ship is setting sail.*

The last month had turned into a cyclone as I realized how unprepared I was for the daily interrogations from everyone. There were many who felt entitled to instruct me on how to execute my spontaneous move, as if the constant apologizing and defending my decision weren't exhausting enough.

The greatest challenge had been listening to people blurt out unsupportive phrases like, "Why? I don't get it," or "You know what you should do…" I also heard a lot of "You won't like it there," "You'll move back soon," "How can you do this to us?" or simply, "Aren't you scared?" In fairness, they didn't know that I was simply answering a calling.

Despite all the contention from everyone, everything else seemed to be falling into place in a fated fashion. A few days after the decision to move to Chicago was finalized, I heard from someone that I hadn't seen in years. She came out for a visit and told me she was moving to LA and needed to furnish her whole place.

Well, how convenient. I just happened to have a fully furnished two-bedroom apartment to get rid of—with limited time to handle that task. Talk about perfect timing. I gave her a generous offer, and she agreed to come back at the end of the month to take everything off my hands.

The timing had also worked out flawlessly for my other friend who was visiting to help with the move and the drive. He had just returned from vacation and was about to start a new work season, so he had a small window of opportunity. Again, how convenient. With their help, we loaded up the U-Haul truck in record time, and it all fit together like a strategic game of Tetris.

We decided to get a good night's sleep, and just as we started to drift off, my stereo system turned on by itself. It was quietly playing the song "Here in Heaven."

My friends weren't the first witnesses of my disruptive lifestyle. This had been occurring for many weeks yet didn't happen once when my ex was living there. Every night before bed, I would turn off the lights and music would come blasting on at the highest volume. It never turned on when the lights were on, and it had never played softly. One night, it even came on three times in a row. It was at different times each night and played stations I didn't listen to—which ruled out the alarm explanation.

As I lay there in bed, I reflected on the conversation from earlier that evening. We had discussed my haunted home from my childhood and my experiences with paranormal activity throughout my life. I told them about the doors that would slam shut, things that mysteriously moved, the TV turning on or

12

pausing by itself, the electronics that malfunctioned and even the piano that played on its own.

I also shared stories about *knowing* or sensing something before it happened—even death. It was the first time I had ever brought it up with anyone outside my family, as it's clearly a vulnerable topic. It was hard to tell them more than that because I didn't understand it. *What does this mean? Why can I feel what other people are feeling and thinking? Why do I hear whispers of guidance or warning? And why is my stereo screaming at me?*

I was relieved that I had finally talked about it, but I was still just as confused as ever. It had always made me feel so *weird*. In search of answers, my mind raced its way into the depths of exhaustion. *Wow, see you soon, Chicago!*

4

BREAKING FREE

My eyes ripped open the next morning before the alarm went off as if a gun had just fired. As I got ready, I didn't recognize myself in the mirror. Focusing was impractical. Each step required calculated thought, or I might just float away. *Am I really doing this?*

It was all in slow motion. Part of me was already in Chicago, as my eagerness to prove this to myself, and my skeptical audience, only grew. Parting with my old life, I peeled away in a haze of disorientation. All anchors had been cut—the ship was officially sailing. *Do I know how to sail, though?*

I don't think I had ever been so exhilarated yet scared in my life. *Seriously? What am I doing?* Had I really just walked away from my lovely life with nothing more than what fit in my little two-door car?

I forced myself to relax my shoulders and sit back into the

seat. My body language was definitely not screaming cool, calm, and collected. It was like going on a blind date but already committing to moving in. *Think positively. Now please get your face off the steering wheel. Remember, if you lead the body, the mind will naturally follow. Just stay calm, listen to your instincts—and chill out, chica!*

With some inner reassurance, the noise of my self-defeating fears began to subside. There was deep-rooted faith that this was the right direction and that it was time to let go and ride the wave. The adrenaline was the only fuel in me, and it was a full tank. *I'm free. No rules!*

The windows were down, and the music was turned up, allowing my mind to wander as I reflected on the vision board I had recently created. Images of my deepest desires had been e-mailed to myself so that everything was dated and documented. Curiosity about how this attraction experiment would unfold was inevitable.

The fire to reach my dreams was roaring. My plan to get it all was to master the Law of Attraction, since the greatest teachers, philosophers, and leaders throughout history were aware of its power and truth. Who am I to argue with that? From past experiences, I was already a believer.

This time, however, I was in the market for a whole new life—a life that I was visualizing coming together in just seventy-two hours. I needed some serious proof. *What if it doesn't work this time? What if I don't want to stay there? What if I don't make friends? What if I can't find a job? Ahh, stop that!*

Retraining my way of thinking required constant mental focus. *Remember, everything in life comes back to energy and the mind. Only send positive energy toward it, and don't let those doubts nullify positive energy frequencies. Feel how it will feel. Give gratitude and trust that it will lead you to where you need to be.*

Thoughts of being single, dating, and writing—while having a thriving social life—in my beautiful city apartment consumed me. Anonymity was calling my name as I drove toward my future. It was time for an unforgettable summer. My thoughts bounced around in an entertaining fashion, as they danced with visions of my future self.

Time was exhilaratingly irrelevant. I had resisted the urge to plan any details. This was a nauseating leap of faith, and I was free-falling. As both scientist and subject of this wacky experiment, I was impatient for the results.

Things had been nothing but planned my whole life, an endless game of filling up all the white squares in my planner—documented proof of my overly committed existence. *How free are we when our time seems to belong to everything and everyone else, as we often put our own desires and dreams on the back burner to appease others?*

The magnitude of my freedom was causing realizations to surface. I thought about *the* book that I had always known I would write since I was a little girl. It was swimming around inside of me in the depths of encrypted chaos. *How am I going to get this thing out of me? It's just a scattered jigsaw puzzle in my mind. Where do I start?*

I had attempted to write it many times, but it had only been shoved to the side in frustration. *What am I supposed to write about? Who would want to read that? What do I know?* All I knew was that it was time to figure it out.

I was anxious to see Chicago for the first time. Would *we* have chemistry? Would the love be reciprocated? Many hours had been spent picturing Chicago welcoming me with open arms—not even knowing exactly what that meant. Would I get the welcoming *hug* I ached for so badly? *How do I already love this mysterious city?*

The restraints fell off as the miles accumulated behind me. I had parted with my apartment, my responsibilities, and the majority of my possessions. I had quit my jobs, sadly left my friends, and closed the door on a former version of myself. It was foreign yet completely innate.

No matter what happened next, the dramatic inner shift was irreversible. I had somehow shed an unwanted layer of myself. *Thank you, Universe. I surrender. My life is in your hands. Good thing I trust you!*

5

READY, SET, GO...

My face welcomed the early morning sun as the last few hours of the drive gently washed over me. Anticipation flooded my body as the moment of truth neared. There was no turning back. There was no backup plan. Not knowing the fate of what lay ahead had my stomach in my throat. *What am I doing?*

Fortunately, the moment the city came into view, infatuation dominated the doubts. How could a skyline cause such an emotional reaction? Was it too soon to call it home? Would the energy that was charging every cell in my body continue? *Wow, this feels so right.*

There wasn't time to allow the fear and discomfort to slow me down, although I was highly cognizant of their looming presence. *I made it. Wow, this place has unbelievable energy. It's the perfect place to reboot, rebuild, and grow.*

The clock had started. In seventy-two hours, my new life

would become tangible—but how? That was for the Universe to piece together. My role was to listen to my inner guidance and take inspired action. I had spread my wings and was reveling in the fresh air. The possibilities were limitless.

There was inevitable concern about finding an apartment, because I had a tall order to fill. I was in search of a flexible sublet in a safe area that was also fully furnished and without a roommate—again, tall order.

◊

The next morning, the realtor showed me several apartments in the downtown area. My instincts weren't agreeing with the unfurnished, impersonal, and limited space this area had to offer, or the lack of parking. My gut was tightening with resistance.

I inquired about other apartments, and he offered to show me some more the following week. However, waiting around for a potential place while racking up nights at a hotel just wasn't going to work either. Anxiety was starting to storm on my celebratory party. *I need to get a place sooner than that. Please help me, Universe.*

Just as I was about to politely decline my realtor's offer, his phone rang. When he finished with his call, he told me that his next appointment had just canceled, and he suggested that we head toward the other apartments right then and there. *How convenient.*

As soon as we arrived, I reactively heated up on the inside. My anxiety was replaced with euphoric bliss again. He had led me right to the area I wanted to live in. Even though the apartments did not fit my needs, it was still confirmation that I was on the right track.

So began the apartment search. I typed in the area I wanted and searched for furnished places within my budget. Of the twelve search results, only two didn't require a year lease, and both were less than optimal. With a comparable Carrie Bradshaw lifestyle in mind, a frat boy reality show wasn't going to cut it. *Where am I supposed to live?*

"Relax. It will work out."

That was deeply known. So the rest of the day was solely reserved for walking around in a state of mixed gratitude and disbelief. Standing in awe looking at the architecture of the city and the beauty of Lake Michigan, I just wanted to hug everyone who walked by. *I love you, and I love you—and yup, I love you too. Wow, I'm finally here.*

My state was an identical match to a kid at an amusement park. Aware of the bounce in my step, there was no wiping away the massive grin. Then it was back to the room to get ready.

"Do the search again."

Okie dokie! Sure enough, a gorgeous condo was now available—and it fit my criteria flawlessly. One glance at the interior, and I knew it was going to be my home. I sent a quick e-mail to the owner expressing my eagerness to see the place. This was *my* condo, and it was love at first sight.

After a night of delicious food and soulful blues, an e-mail from the owner's boyfriend explained that his girlfriend was currently on her way home from Japan. There were many people who were interested, several of whom had already seen the place and were coming back to look a second time. He offered to show it to me the next day—with no guarantees, of course.

He only had the early morning open, so that's what we agreed on. I started jumping up and down on the bed—I *knew* it was mine. I fell asleep smiling. *Thank you, Universe. Thank you for my new home!*

6

TIME'S UP

The next morning, my conviction to get that apartment ripped me out of a deep sleep. The forty-eight-hour mark was looming close by. Sure, it didn't seem like the odds were in my favor, but I just *knew* this was destined to work out. "Thank you" kept repeating in my head the whole drive over there, and I visualized myself unpacking that evening.

It had mentally registered as my home before I even stepped through the front door. Then the kitchen took my breath away as I noticed the uncanny similarities to my previous visualizations. The beautiful, oversized countertop in the kitchen practically had a welcome sign on it.

It was fully furnished, with high ceilings, a fireplace, and a garage. The Universe certainly got my order right and even threw in some extra bonuses. It was easy to envision myself making a fire, dancing on the hardwood floors, and sitting at the countertop writing and reading all night. I could practically smell my first meal and couldn't wait to start cooking. It truly was a comparable "Carrie Bradshaw apartment"—and a writer's dream.

The owner informed me that the person she had wanted to rent to hadn't worked out because she had been in Japan when the tenant was available to sign the paperwork. Now she was back, but that same potential tenant was unexpectedly out of town for the next week. *Hmm, how convenient!*

Due to this, she decided she would go with someone else who was willing to sign that day. It was in high demand, so she also wanted four months in advance. The paperwork was signed quickly, and the keys to my new place were collected. It was very obvious that if I had not been the first showing that morning, someone else would have snatched it up. It was meant to be.

Once she left, I darted outside to start learning my new neighborhood. The first stop was a breakfast place a few blocks away. I went straight to the counter to enjoy an omelet and freshly squeezed juice. While sitting there oozing positive energy, a friendly looking guy with an infectious smile started talking to me.

There was an instant soul recognition when I met "Phab Phil," and within just a few sentences, we were calling each other "instafriends" and making plans to hang out (it's probably not a mystery what his sexual orientation is). That's right: I now had the beautiful city apartment for writing *and* a cosmic gay best friend.

The next step was to empty my jam-packed car and locate the nearest grocery store. I practically floated home with my groceries, and my face hurt from the maniac smile I had stopped trying to control. *I can't believe I live here. I can't believe this is my life. Thank you!*

Some hidden reserves of energy surfaced as the job search began. Almost immediately, I saw a listing for the one job that I had mentioned before moving. I couldn't believe it.

The hours were slipping away as I danced around in a victorious rhythm, my head in the clouds. *Wow, if we can use our minds to do anything, then can't we change this world? Can't we make that change through intention and co-creating with the Universe? Aren't we more powerful than we are aware of and have been conditioned to believe? This is what we should be teaching our children! They need to know that anything is possible!*

In the midst of my euphoric daze, I checked my e-mail and discovered that I was being asked to interview tomorrow at the place I wanted to work at. The address revealed that it was just a short walking distance away. My head kept shaking in disbelief. *Wow, this is incredible! I love the Law of Attraction!*

The next morning, I imagined that this was my daily walk to work and that I would breeze through the interview. I was informed that the only reason the position was even open was because a person who was recently hired didn't show up for their first day. *Again, how convenient!*

The "coincidences" were stacking up. There was an undeniable sense that the Universe was bending and twisting in my favor. The energy was palpable. The position was offered to me on the spot, and then I connected with some of the employees. There was no denying that it was going to be a highly social summer.

I now had a completely different life, as if it had just been waiting there for me, like a parallel universe. These results were undeniable and crucial to my experiment.

To top it off, as I walked home, I stopped somewhere and ended up meeting a guy that I had instant chemistry with. After talking for a while, I agreed to hang out with him again. *Now you're just showing off, Universe!*

It had only been one week since I had packed up my apartment, loaded up my car, and drove off—and only three full days since arriving in Chicago. It was exactly what I had intended to do. The seventy-two hours were up. The clock ran out just as everything fell into place, literally down to the hour.

It had all happened in record time. It was now just hitting me. *Wow, I love my new home. I can't believe I got the job I wanted. I'm so excited for my social plans. My new friends are amazing, and how am I already completely settled? I did it! This is unreal!*

The rest of the night was for isolated reflection and pure relaxation. Nothing seemed real. If I had suddenly woken up in my bed in Sonoma, it wouldn't have shocked me. Until then though, I had every intention of enjoying the dream. There were no rules. No schedule. No social demands. No sense of time. The accumulated fear faded as I gave into the decompression.

Sitting at my countertop with soulful music playing, candles burning, and a home-cooked salmon dinner triggered the tears of relief. Experiencing such an intense spectrum of emotions the last few months finally caught up with me. *Wow, it's all behind me—like it never happened.*

My head shook in disbelief as the positive force field around me amplified exponentially. *How did this all happen? How did so many "coincidences" guide me straight to the lifestyle I had been dreaming of? If this is possible, what else can I accomplish? What can humanity accomplish if we get more creative with world peace and utilize the collective consciousness?*

So many people, circumstances, gut feelings, and random acts of precise timing had guided me to everything I had wanted, as if the whole thing had been carefully orchestrated. The Chicago version of myself wasn't just a figment of my imagination anymore. She was in full form, and wow was she happy. *See, we do think our lives into existence. That is simply amazing! How liberating!*

The imaginary clock had run out, just before the seventy-two-hour mark, and my life was better than I could have imagined. There was officially something to this whole attraction thing and this was clearly just the start of proving that. *Let the fun continue!*

7

THE SUMMER OF INDULGENCE

Upon validating Chicago's reputation for sinfully good food, it became apparent that this was going to be the summer of indulgence, and that was fine by me. The Chicago sitcom continued.

I was now exclusively seeing the guy I had met within the seventy-two-hour mark. This time, however, the relationship wasn't romanticized. I cared about him, of course, but refrained from allowing the emotions to rule me—a title never occurred to me. Not worrying about where it was going, and allowing it to just be, was truly empowering. In other words, he wasn't my identity; he was just a piece of my world.

My "instafriend," Phil, and I continued to explore our effortless bond. He was the person I opened up to the most, as he was always positive and supportive. We often joked about how a woman just needs to date her gay soul mate and then have a lover on the side. Considering how happy our time together made us, it was an idea to consider.

We spent the summer doing things like listening to blues music while sipping on chocolate martinis. I would show up at his house, and he would have chocolate-covered strawberries and wine ready for us. He understood the importance of slowing down and heightening the senses. *Ahh, I love a good romantic.*

Our *dates* were enchanting and unforgettable. We were always able to get lost in the moment, slow and in the flow of the Universe. We never planned anything. We just went with the wind and arrived where it carried us. Sometimes we would start walking in a direction with no destination in mind and end up with a jam-packed night full of memories.

One night, Phil mentioned that he had entered a drawing for tickets to the Conan O'Brien show in Chicago. When I got home, I entered without telling him. I imagined winning the tickets and gave gratitude for being able to go. *I feel a win coming on!*

Sure enough, a couple weeks later he told me that he had not won, and I surprised him with two tickets to Conan and a day of city exploration.

What was even more amazing was that the show was at the Chicago Theatre, which just happened to be on my vision board. A heated flash of energy zipped through me when I originally saw that image, and now winning tickets to go there was confirming why. *Wow, that was a powerful coincidence! I seriously love the Law of Attraction.*

That same week, I was handed two free tickets to see the Cubs play the Red Sox. They were only in town for a three-day interleague game for the first time in years, and the two days I went just happened to be the two days that they won. Those were the only free tickets I received all summer, and the Red Sox were also on my vision board.

Outside of work, I made plenty of time to enjoy the perfection that is summer in Chicago. It was a magical whirl of street festivals, bike rides along Lake Michigan, beach volleyball, brewery visits, comedy shows, exploration, live music, improvisation shows, boating, sinful food, constant play, and epic people watching.

It was incredible to acknowledge that this life-changing experience only happened because of overpowering fear, trusting my instincts and taking a leap of faith. *I'm so grateful I sailed my way into this harbor.* However, unknown to me, some dark clouds were about to roll in.

8

CHANGE OF PLANS

Even with all the fun, the silence of my home was the thing I most desired. I was lost in my studies, just waiting to hear if I was accepted into the Psychology of Organizational Leadership Program.

The wrestling match with my book continued as the stack of research and ideas continued to grow—but the words didn't flow. *How can I pass along wisdom in a unique way when it's all so knotted within me?*

I immersed myself in neuro-linguistic programming, human behavior, and anything that had to do with the mind, especially subconscious reprogramming. My focus was on conquering the anxiety that had plagued me for years. *I have to find a way to be comfortable in my body! I'm tired of feeling electrocuted all the time.*

For months, I had been envisioning myself getting into school and skipping over the anxiety-provoking interview. After meeting with someone in admissions, I learned that they didn't let people skip that process.

So the gratitude revved up, as did the determination. I specifically focused on calling my parents and saying, "I got accepted, and they let me skip the interviewing process." I pre-experienced the celebratory emotions behind that call.

Sure enough, a phone call a couple weeks later revealed an acceptance, without the need for an interview. That was a really proud call home. This visualizing thing was really working. It was unbelievable to feel so in control of my life. *We really are the creators of our own destiny. Talk about empowering!*

However, despite my eagerness to start school, it didn't take long to sense that something was wrong. As soon as I started classes, a deep heaviness filled my stomach as the reality hit me—I wasn't free anymore.

My positive energy vanished, as I was now trapped inside writing papers about theories that didn't excite me. It was back to the academic world after years of thinking freely. Now there wasn't time to study what I was truly passionate about—like my enticing stack of books that was being neglected. I watched my enthusiasm for life, and my creativity, instantly suffer.

This was a three-year program that only allowed for a few weeks off a year. This meant no traveling because that limited time off would be for family and friends. It would mean that my attraction experiment would be put on the back burner. The idea of turning down my passion thermometer just wasn't resonating. In fact, it was breaking my spirit.

There was a nuclear war going on inside of me, and I was ready to combust at any moment. I was, again, a prisoner of my own life. Trapped. *Something feels wrong. Very wrong! I can't breathe. What should I do?*

To amplify my stress, my landlord announced an engagement. This wouldn't have been a big deal, but she wanted to remodel the condo before everyone flew in for the ceremony next month. So this meant I had to be out in just a few weeks. *Next month? Why rush commitment? I'm not ready to leave!*

My heavenly summer had taken an unforeseen twist. My head was spinning, and there was no one to turn to for help. Wanting to stay through the end of September meant another two months. How was I going to find a place that fast that also fit my needs for just two months? The walls were closing in.

A solution was needed immediately. There was a pit in my stomach that I couldn't ignore, and it matched the twisted look on my face. I loved my life. I didn't want to change it. Where would I live? What should I do about school? *I can't drop out of school—can I?*

"Drop out of school."

I had always believed that a PhD was necessary to have credibility. Did I really need it, though? Could I become a leader without that piece of paper to grant my worthiness? I had worked so hard to get in. This had been a tedious and time-consuming process the last few months, and it was hard to imagine it being for nothing.

"Drop out of school."

How was I going to tell everyone? Where was I going to live? I wasn't ready to move back to New York yet, where I'm originally from. It was summer in Chicago, and I wanted to savor the rest of it—every drop of it. *Will I be happy if I stay in this program? Seriously, what will everyone think? Am I really considering this?*

"Drop out of school."

Obsessively pacing while weighing the options, I reminded myself to focus on my overall well-being first and foremost. *What would make me the happiest? Freedom makes me happy. Adventure makes me happy. Experience makes me happy. Hmm…*

Then it occurred to me that if I were going to drop out, I would need to make a vow to myself to accomplish something more profound than a degree. This meant I would take the money for school and put that into fulfilling my purpose and dreams. It also meant that I would amp up my exploration for the truth. It meant no rules. *Hmm, that sounds interesting. Very interesting.*

"Drop out of school."

Then it happened: my tormented indecisiveness abruptly resolved itself. *I'm dropping out of school. I'm going to explore and question everything. I'm going to reach my goals. I'm going to take time off for the first time in my life. It's time to become a true writer. For once, I'm not going to care what anyone thinks.*

It was a sudden blast of conviction. Life is an adventure, so I decided to put experience before education. I had just had my fill. I knew there was another way to achieve success—by pursuing my passions. *Phew, I'm still free.*

With school out of the picture, I promised myself to reach my dreams and create something that made a mark in history. At that exact moment, I decided to enroll myself in my own self-imposed PhD program. *I'm going to prove to everyone that our thoughts create our reality. I'm going to help as many people as possible, and I'm going to open myself up to whatever the Universe wants to bring my way.*

Despite my strong conviction that this was the right path, I acknowledged the feelings of foolishness and humiliation at the thought of announcing it to everyone. I had made a big deal about school to hold myself socially accountable, never thinking that I would walk away from it. I thought it was my ticket to success because that's what society had always drilled into my mid.

However, I was seriously questioning what society had led me to believe. Actually, I was questioning a lot of things at this time and starting to examine everything in a new light. *The "real world" is a lot different than everyone makes it seem. It's interesting how conventional thinking seems to be limited thinking, considering we are limitless beings. How strange that the Law of Attraction was never mentioned in school—despite the fact that it's the most empowering thing I've ever learned. That's rather suspicious...*

9

AN UPGRADE

As if deciding about school wasn't draining enough, the clock was ticking on finding a place to live. An online search with my criteria revealed only one place that was a match, although there wasn't a picture of it.

The description explained that the two people currently living there were looking for a two-month sublet because the third roommate was moving to New York for an unexpected job offer. We exchanged some e-mails, and this place remained the only one of consideration for the next couple weeks. *There's that inner twinge of excitement; this must be my new place. I wonder what it looks like.*

Three days later, I pulled up to a two-story penthouse located right near Wrigley Field, just a five-minute walk to work and dangerously close to my favorite Mexican place—the one I had renamed Burrito Heaven.

The place was stunning, and the new roommates were very easygoing. They were supposed to show it to several other people that day, but we sealed the deal, and I began preparing for another move. What had appeared to be awful news about moving out of my apartment had quickly transformed into an upgraded lifestyle and lower rent. It was simply a test of faith.

However, as I was coasting along, enjoying each and every day, *he* came back into my life. I knew not to let him in, but cue my sweet sociopath.

10

MY SWEET SOCIOPATH

We had met quite a few years prior. As convoluted as our story is, our initial meeting was as simple as it gets. Grad school had just wrapped up, and some classmates and I were out to celebrate. I spotted him sitting alone, and I'm convinced the room froze for just a moment. An unprecedented *"There you are"* was whispered from within.

Without any conscious thought, I calmly marched over and positioned myself next to him. Within a flash, we were making eye contact in the mirror, with matching smirks on our faces.

I turned, smiled, and waited for him to initiate. With a boyish grin, he said, "I like your hat." It was basic but shocking considering my conversation from earlier that night. I had just advised some male friends to approach women with a genuine and casual compliment to open up conversation—instead of cheesy pickup lines. The exact example I had provided them was simply, "I like your hat." So that was it for me.

Our connection was effortless, arguably scripted. We were a cosmic fit, and our chemistry could have wiped out a city. We seemed to agree on everything and had all the same interests. We danced and talked all night.

Our time together flew by in a blur of laughter, deep conversation, and long stares as the chemicals releasing in my brain left me mesmerized. He was just so smooth, so sweet, so attentive, and so intriguing. I had never met anyone like him, and I had been single for so long. His charm was disorienting.

The few red flags were swept under the carpet of delusion, leaving me with only one acknowledged concern—that he lived on the other side of the country and was leaving the next day. The timing was additionally unfortunate because I was about to move to Florida. *Really, Universe? I've been single for years, and now you bring a guy into my life when I'm leaving?*

Without so much as a kiss, we embraced in an exaggerated hug and said good-bye. He invited me to hang out the next day, leaving giddiness as my only state of existence.

However, the following day, I had to turn him down because of a bizarre ice skating accident. Having skated my whole life without injury, it was shocking that broken ribs had just set up a roadblock.

We communicated for a while, but maintaining small talk via texting and e-mailing wasn't exactly fulfilling. For the next four years, we were pulled in different directions. We both frequently moved around the country and traveled often; the timing always seemed to be conspiring against us. Of course, I had romanticized the situation, believing that we were being kept apart by mysterious forces until the right time. My romantic nature continued to blur my reality.

There were a number of times that he asked me to drop everything to come visit him, and each time I had to say no because of work commitments. Long distance wasn't for me, especially without a foundation.

Then the few times that we did see each other in New York, we would dance, laugh, and converse as if no time had passed. Once we parted ways though, he was always just out of reach. So I played it cool and never had the courage to ask why he wasn't making more of an effort to be with me. The assumption was that he just wasn't ready, so I didn't push it.

So there he was, contacting me again, out of nowhere. My gut was telling me to be careful, but my heart was taking the reins. Then his excuses didn't take long to cloud my judgment. Of course, he acted like nothing had happened—he always did.

However, something was different this time: he was now saying that he was finally ready. This was the first time he had said he was willing to give *us* a shot, and my heart opened wide and said, "C'mon in," completely bypassing the protective guards that had been strategically put in place. *Welcome back, my charming Casanova. Make yourself at home.*

We started talking regularly, and he repeatedly said, "Hurry home so we can be together"—the exact words I'd been longing to hear from him. This was the first time he had lived in New York since we first met, and he had me convinced that he had grown up and was ready for a serious relationship. I accepted his apologies and fell for his heart-wrenching excuses once again. *Is the timing finally right?*

We continued to make plans for our future—from discussing romantic getaways, to going to baseball games, to carving pumpkins. I couldn't wait to be with him. I foolishly told everyone about what was happening and how *perfect* the timing was. It was as though the curse had been lifted, and we were both on the same wavelength at last. I was finally going to get my *happy* ending.

That summer was a transitional stage in my life that changed me to the core, and Chicago has a permanent place in my heart. As much as I'd love to delve into every detail of my summer of independence, I really must fast forward to heartbreak highway. Hold on tightly because it's a bumpy ride—it certainly made me nauseous. *Good-bye, my lovely Chicago. You changed me, and I thank you!*

11

THE SWITCH

The drive went by in a blur of dreamy fantasies. No matter how much I try to control it, I'm still a self-diagnosed chronic daydreamer. At the same time, I also couldn't stop worrying about two recent dreams about my grandmother, and in both she was crying. In each of them I was assuring her that I was going to be okay.

This might not seem too significant to most, but whenever she had visited me in the past, it was with a strong message that came true shortly afterward. We had been extremely close, and her visitations were always positive. I knew something was wrong, but as my brain released those hazy love drugs, those instinctual concerns were washed away.

Just hours after finishing the drive, he texted me and explained that a work thing had suddenly come up, and he needed to fly to LA immediately. *Uh-oh. That doesn't feel right.*

Every inch of me knew something was off. My body was aggressively alerting me; it was impossible to ignore. I had been trying to silence the whispers of caution that had been bouncing around in my mind over the last few weeks. Those fears were cutting into my ignorant bliss.

My worries were chucked to the side as the storytelling with my family began. We were cozy in the living room when I instinctually stepped away for a quick (and destined) second to see if he had made it safely to California.

Checking his social media, there was a new picture of him with a blonde woman who I had never seen before. She was proclaiming how happy she was to be reunited with her boyfriend of eight months. Who? What! Why was *my* guy with another woman? *Eight months? Gee, I guess he made it there.*

Sitting there in panicked shock, I couldn't cry. I couldn't even think. *What just happened?* Then right at that moment, he deleted the post. He was hiding her! It had all happened so fast. There was an urge to erase it and forget what I had seen. *No, no, no. That's not possible. I can't handle this.*

Then it hit me: How many of us were there? How many women had he been stringing along and hiding from each other? Fate had stepped in—fate that had systematically crushed my whole world. I had ignored my gut feelings and the red flags from over the years. I had been in denial about the dreams with my grandmother. I had ignored my inner warning system.

My family was calling me back to the living room, but I couldn't even comprehend standing up. The wind had been knocked out of me as humiliation filled my stomach and started to harden like cement. *This isn't happening, is it? I can't breathe.*

My mind raced around for answers. He had asked me to come home to be with him. *He has a girlfriend? How? What? Should I tell her?* The irony was that she looked so happy and innocent that I wanted to save her. I couldn't blame her. It wasn't her fault. I decided to say nothing.

Suddenly, my prince was more grotesque than any living creature in existence. Now that the veil had been lifted, I became aware of how much he had been torturing me for years and how blinded I was. He had been punishing me by repeatedly disappearing for not giving him what he wanted: spur-of-the-moment trips to see him and, of course, sex—which I was now so grateful for.

He wasn't used to people not being obedient. So he would swoop back in to secure me a seat on his nauseating emotional roller coaster, and I would fasten myself in. He had a hold on me—a big one.

As each of his lies became crystal clear in my mind, each passing minute blasted me like a surprise missile attack. The glaring red flags had been ignored, and I had been demolished because of it.

What was I going to tell everyone? Had he ever meant a word he had said to me? What was I going to do now? How could I ever trust anyone again? *I can't survive this. Where are my tears? Where did all the oxygen go? Wow, I feel so stupid.*

The floor was shifting beneath me as my bugged-out eyes alerted my family that something was very wrong. Everything went numb as I suffocated from shame. I wanted to hide under a rock (or beat him with one).

The rage was building, but I didn't know if it was directed more toward him or myself. With a blank stare, the same phrase repeated over and over: "I can't survive this." The disgust and self-blame were drowning me. There was no backup plan, and I was clearly in shock. *Will I ever be able to take a full breath? Did I really have to put those blinders on again?*

Then, without warning, it happened: The Switch. Suddenly the self-defeating chatter in my brain stopped, and a commanding voice took over, saying, *NO! You can rise above this. Get up!*

Something primal and fierce flipped over inside of me, and I *knew* that he wasn't allowed to waste more of my time. I couldn't give a monster that much power—especially a cowardly monster who had wormed his way in to intentionally hurt me.

This was an unprecedented defense mechanism, which showed up just in time. Thankfully, there was only a two-week wait before my first major distraction, a trip to Asia that had been booked as soon as I walked away from school.

My priorities shifted once again. It became evident that the best revenge was to reach my desires, and he was going to be the fuel for my fire. Now able to do whatever I wanted—there were absolutely no anchors—I was, again, heading out to open waters. *Phew, I dodged another bullet. Good-bye, my sweet sociopath—and thank you for lighting me up!*

12

THE PSYCHIC IN THE BACK

To further my attraction experiment, I watched the DVD *The Secret* every night for a week because I wanted it ingrained in my mind. *People do know that this is quantum physics, and it's a universal law, not a theory, right? It's kind of a big deal—it can change anyone's life. It can change our world. How can I help teach this?*

It was just a couple days before heading out to L.A., which was my first stop before San Francisco and ultimately Asia. For some reason, a nagging feeling to join my parents on their date wouldn't let up. They had a gift certificate and were looking forward to a romantic night out. *Well, this is odd. Why am I trying to be the third wheel?*

I had never been to that restaurant but just *knew* I was supposed to go with them. After some persistence, we decided to call it my going-away dinner. *Well, this has an interesting energy around it.*

So the next day, my mom and I were out for a walk before dinner, and I looked at her and randomly blurted out, "I need to see a psychic, and I need to work on my meditation." Neither of which I had ever done. *Where did that come from?*

Going to a medium for a reading made me curious, so getting a message to do it was certainly intriguing. However, I had no idea what I was hoping to accomplish or how to choose a legitimate one. *I wonder if it would work? People tend to dismiss and discredit them. I'm only interested in the truth. Why the strong feeling?*

My inner voice had also nudged me to start meditating recently, and imagining myself doing that on the beach was definitely appealing. However, I had no idea how to do it. I wasn't convinced that my mind could slow down enough to benefit from it.

Our walk in the park was peaceful as we appreciated the fall leaves and the flawless weather. My mom and I chatted excitedly about my upcoming trip. Then suddenly, in a quick swoop, my energy was sucked right out of me. Just like that, I had gone from bursting with energy to zapped into zombie mode. *Whoa, where is my soul?*

My eyelids instantly gained weight as I struggled to keep them open. I began feeling disoriented and lethargic, beyond a post-massage feeling. My focus was wrecked, and I kept repeating, "I feel like an empty shell." *What is this?*

After apologizing several times to my mom for being so out of it, we both realized it was something far beyond my control or understanding. I kept saying, "My soul just left. I'm just a body right now." *What is going on? What just happened to me?*

Then as I approached the front of the restaurant, I was blasted by a restored strength right at the door. It smacked me in the face and surged through me, as though the switch had just been turned back on. I was even forced to take a step back and reorient myself from the wave of energy. *How weird!*

As drastic as it was, I didn't put too much thought into it because I simply didn't get it—that, and I was hungry. So we found my dad and got seated and quickly decided on our order.

Looking around the restaurant, I couldn't help but notice a gathering of women by the back bar. Something told me to ask my server about it, and I was told that it was a bachelorette party that had hired a psychic. *Seriously? I just mentioned a psychic. How random.*

Without even hesitating, I asked to buy a reading from her. He returned shortly with apologies and explained that it was a private party, so no one else could get a reading. *Then why do I feel like I'm about to get one?*

Shortly afterward, the owner came over. She had heard about my interest in getting a reading and said she could arrange for that to happen. She also informed us that six out of the seven women who had a reading returned crying because she was so accurate.

My skeptical side knew proof was necessary. I decided to cover up my ring finger so she couldn't see my marital status— painfully single. I also instructed myself to not react with emotion or to give any clues. This was my first reading, and to be convinced would require a lot.

Despite my guarded composure, she saw right through me. Actually, she barely looked at me. Dawn tilted her head to the side, and facts about my life just came pouring out of her mouth. She mentioned specific people who had passed away, and she knew about the white horse I helped take care of from my childhood. She also knew of my single status and that a guy had recently hurt me severely. She emphasized that I had to release the trapped pain.

It was surprising that she knew all my grandparents had passed away. She then blurted out the words, "It was your grandmother who slowed the car down." I had never told anyone outside of my family about that. The only reason I was still alive was that a couple years prior, the most random thing had slowed my car down, causing me to just barely avoid a fatal accident.

An angel figurine had fallen into my lap with the message, *"Never drive faster than your angel can fly."* I slammed on the brakes, and as I turned the corner, I swerved and just missed crashing into a double-decker van that was flipped over in my lane. It had all happened in a split second. The angel had been a gift from her, and instinctually I knew she had saved my life.

Dawn predicted a lot of traveling in the next year. She also talked about the book and said that I was going to help a lot of people and that it was going to be as big as I thought it would be. She then stated that I was about to go to a place where there were beaches and said, "You need to work on your meditation." My head was officially spinning.

As the reading came to an end, I choked back tears and gave her a heartfelt hug. She had spoken directly to my soul, even though she had only talked with me for five minutes. I was now convinced that there are, in fact, accurate psychics.

Right before I walked away, she told me she had *known* she was going to meet someone "special" that day and had felt the energy of it earlier. She then said it was ironic that it was the last person from the party whom she had tapped into.

I clued her into the fact that I was actually just a customer at the restaurant, and she laughingly replied with, "Well, I was supposed to meet you today." *Okay, this must have to do with the depletion and then zap of energy from earlier. I don't get it, but I believe it was for a purpose. This is all beyond my comprehension. This is kind of wacky.*

13

OPRAH IS WAITING FOR ME

The night before I left, I received a call from my friend Jessica, who had purchased all my furniture in Sonoma. She was calling to tell me that she had just won two tickets to the Women's Convention the next day. Apparently, there were thousands of people going, but only fifty people had won. *Awesome, but wait—my flight doesn't arrive until tomorrow night.*

"Change your flight."

Hmm, I don't know. Jessica then proceeded to tell me that the Oprah Winfrey Network was hosting it and that Oprah would be there, among many other names I recognized. That changed everything, and I perked right up.

You see, when I was a little girl, I said, "Mom, I'm going to help a lot of people, I'm going to write a book, and I'm going to meet Oprah one day," with several other predictions and complete conviction. Spontaneous by nature, it didn't take much for me to comply.

Now, I want to paint this picture very clearly because, in my mind, I was on my way to *meet* Oprah. (I told you I'm a chronic daydreamer.) With an overpacked bag; a big, clunky computer strapped across my chest; and a giddy smile, power walking toward Oprah was the only focus. For some reason, this *had* to be done in heels, an impractical decision considering the blisters that were now forming.

Still in my hyper state, there was a quick stop in the restroom before catching a cab. I slipped my phone into my back pocket and managed to cram all my stuff in the stall. It all happened in slow motion, and I was just a second too late. Yup, the phone plunged right into the toilet. *Perfect.* Nothing was going to stop me though.

After doing the obvious, I repeatedly tried to get the phone to turn on. It was completely lifeless though. I knew the event was at the LA Convention Center, but that was all I knew. *You've gotta be kidding me!*

The ridiculously priced cab dropped me off in front of the convention center, and I wrestled with my luggage, limping toward the security guards. *Wait...security guards? Are they checking for badges?*

As in the one that I didn't have because the plan had been to call my friend upon arrival so she could bring it to me? *Now I have no phone, and I don't know her number. Wonderful—a classic jam to start the vacation.*

It took some groveling, but I convinced the guards to let me in to talk to the help desk. They said they could let me in the lobby but not into the actual event. Well, I knew that wouldn't work. Nothing was going to stop me from seeing Oprah and, of course, finding my friend. They ended up letting me in with my luggage left behind as collateral. *How hard could it be to find her?*

My temporary badge got me through the doors, and then the realization of how bad the situation was set in. There were mobs of people, and I could barely walk. The anxiety was only amplifying my clumsy mistake. This was my first time staying with Jessica, and I didn't know her address or other people in the area. There was no backup plan to find her. Apparently, I had relied far too much on my phone. *Genius preparation!*

The panic increased, so I went back out to the lobby to reassess. My feet were screaming at me, and I was screaming at myself for messing things up so badly. *What is wrong with me? When will I learn?* So I gave up. I threw my head back and looked up. *Please let me find her. Please let me find her. Please let me find her.*

As a last-ditch effort, I walked back into the entrance area of the event. Only this time, she was casually standing there. Relief blasted me. Then we didn't skip a beat. *Phew!*

We spent the day listening to, and meeting, people like Dr. Phil, Dr. Laura Berman, Deepak Chopra, Gayle King, Martha Beck, members of Oprah's staff, and many other people who are in the line of work that I feel destined for—and equally terrified of.

I studied their speaking styles, pitch, tonality, stage presence, confidence, body language, and ability to engage the audience. *How do they do this? How do they stay so calm? Why do I have such a strong feeling that I'm supposed to end up on stage too? There is no way I can do that; my anxious body won't allow me to. This is scarier than death to me.*

Finally after much anticipation, Ms. Oprah walked out on stage. Her energy flooded the room. Tears filled my eyes. There was the woman I had just jumped hurdles to see. *Wow, no forgetting this moment—worth it!* I visualized meeting her in person.

As we left, I pulled out a copy of *OWN* magazine from the gift bag, and my mouth flopped open. She was on the cover wearing a red dress—an almost identical match to the picture of her on my vision board. I practically had the *Indiana Jones* theme song playing in my head. *Go, Law of Attraction! You're awesome, and I'm your biggest fan!*

At the same time, my mind couldn't turn off the ongoing torment of figuring out what area to specialize in with neuro-linguistic programming (NLP), which I had recently become certified in. There was a pull toward a focus in dating and relationships, but who was I to talk about that? My dating record was lame, at best. *So now what? How is this done? What are the steps? Is this my purpose?*

My marketing friends expected me to know how to put myself out there, but I was a deer in headlights. *How do I show people who I am? What can I say that's different? I certainly know I'm not an expert yet. Choose a niche? Self-start? Okay, well, I'm clueless about how to do that. This is so overwhelming.*

This was a whole new language. One of the terms I had repeatedly stumbled across was "pickup artist." *What in the world is that, and why are people telling me that I need to know about it if I'm getting into dating coaching?*

Then I really started looking into what this mysterious pickup artist community had been up to. Aha! They had been studying things like NLP, human behavior, attraction, social dynamics, and seduction. Of course, their intentions strongly differed from mine, but the truth is the truth, and they had found it.

Even though these were some of my areas of study, I was wildly intimidated by everything and sensed the amateur spotlight was on me. There was so much to learn and so many techniques to test. It was so foreign. *Just keep going, whatever that means.*

Many people in the dating community repeatedly recommended that I read *The Game* by Neil Strauss. *Who's that? Okay, well, I will add that to my skyscraper stack of books.* In the meantime, my focus was solely on my dream vacation. *Yay! This is going to be life-changing! I can feel it!*

14

FELLOW DREAM CHASER

It had been years since we had seen each other, so it was strange that I had the urge to contact him in the first place. We had worked together and then both relocated, naturally losing touch. Now we were randomly meeting at the San Francisco airport.

Of course, when I saw him, the comfort level picked up right where we had left off. That's what's cool about Zach: he's just easy to be around. Something was very different about him, though. He looked like he was in shock, but in a good way. It was obvious that something had blown his mind, and he was struggling to process it.

Zach didn't waste a second with small talk, and he started telling me one of the most passionate and compelling stories I had ever heard. It was clear that he was looking for someone to share in his excitement. I was all-ears, as my own journey had only just started—and I love a great story!

The rush-hour traffic was actually serving us as Zach drove on autopilot and tried to relay the insanity of his story. His eyes were bugged out of his head and he spoke quickly, as if there wasn't enough time to explain what had happened to him. *How did he do this? How did he reach his dreams?*

He explained that for the last three years, he had been chasing a dream that people in his life didn't understand. It wasn't practical or conventional, and he didn't care. He just knew he wanted to be a professional photographer for the world's top surfers. He wound up broke three times as he "irrationally" invested in every opportunity to even sit in the back of the room, watching people who did what he wanted to do. *Wow, how inspiring.*

He explained the Universe's itinerary of tests, challenges, and painful lessons. It was all a test of his faith, and he never lost sight of what he wanted. He just held on tight.

In fact, for years he kept showing up and got involved in any way he could. He would pay guys just to go out with them on their jet skis. Now it was finally paying off for him. His whole life had changed because he'd captured the number one photo of Kelly Slater when he won the title, and it ended up in *Sports Illustrated.*

His exuberant energy was contagious, and my highly sensitive nervous system was soaring on his vibrations. He was radiating heat, and I wanted to feel that in response to my own dreams coming true. I ached to feel that for myself. *I have to experience the natural high that he's feeling. I have to feel success at that level! I have to!*

Between Oprah and Zach, my motivation level was fully charged, and I knew that reaching my dreams was the only option. I visualized my eyes bugged out of my head in blissful excitement, my mind blown with self-gratification. *I want to love what I do!*

With only a large, scattered pile of ideas and research for my book, it was becoming evident that more than one book was swarming around within me. In fact, there were a few. They were so massively tangled that my head just shook with bafflement at the idea of separating them. *I have to become an original author. How can I do this? It's like a ten-million-piece puzzle, and I can't even connect two pieces.*

Eventually, he dropped me off in Sonoma, and we parted ways. A sacred inner vow to face my fears and co-create my dreams with the Universe was made at a level that startled me. My fiery passion had just been fueled as a self-promise to never give up, no matter how hard things became, sealed the deal. *Okay, Universe. Let the journey continue—in Vietnam, of course!*

15

WELCOME TO VIETNAM

With a sigh of relief, Karin and I snagged our luggage and exited the terminal, stepping into a mob of welcome signs. We were all shoulder to shoulder and bumping into each other in hopes of finding the piece of paper with our names on it—a disorienting game, considering our state of mind. This was the first time I ever had a driver waiting for me after a flight, and relief to flee the mob scene was undeniable. *I can't believe I'm in Vietnam!*

Jamie's energy greeted me before we even stopped the car, our connection already established. She had an angelic aura (something I don't say often—in fact, almost never). The magical vacation had officially begun.

There were gifts and snacks waiting for us on the bed in the guest room. The generosity comforted my sore heart.

The next morning, Jamie provided us with a list of various activities. We decided to explore the city on Vespas, so we rented two of them and each sat on the back as our tour guides showed us around.

We couldn't stop giggling as we wove through jam-packed crowds of people. It was absolutely exhilarating. The scene became more dramatic as heavy rain started to pour on us, but that certainly didn't stop us. My eyes just closed with emotionally charged mindfulness, and an inner prayer for safety.

Just a few weeks prior, I was living in Chicago and about to start a life with someone on the East Coast. Now I was on the other side of the world, knowing I was completely done with him and ruling out the idea of settling down—or even dating, for that matter. More inspired than ever, it became obvious that this was going to be a wild journey, with limitless possibilities ahead.

Over the next couple of weeks, we traveled to different places as our generous hosts introduced a surreal lifestyle. There were custom-made dresses, extravagant dinners, a first-class trip to a resort in Da Nang, massages, pedicures, and cozy accommodations, which involved afternoons of leisurely reading by the pool. We also attended a yoga instruction and a local cooking class with people from around the world.

The Asian culture has always deeply resonated with me on a multitude of levels, so being there to heal was a spiritual blessing. However, even with a dramatic smile on my face, the numbness within couldn't be ignored. *I can't believe I let him hurt me like that. Why do I have to lead with my heart?*

On one particular day, Jamie took us to an orphanage where she volunteered as a dance teacher. As we pulled up, a group of girls raced to our car and greeted us with nothing but unconditional love, big smiles, and warm embraces. Their joyful welcome was infectious. My heart burst with love.

As we entered the building, the living conditions were alarming. The run-down building, the thick stench, the stagnant heat, the cramped living situations, the dirty clothes—the cockroach that just scurried across the bathroom floor. It was all so shocking and painful to take in. The unfairness of it all wasn't easy to process. *Maybe people should turn off their TVs and start seeing how other people live—the true reality show. I feel sick.*

Despite the less-than-ideal environment we were in, we all laughed and danced as if we were at summer camp. We were drenched in sweat, and I'm surprised I didn't faint.

Afterward, we continued to explore the city. My heart broke further as I witnessed the local poverty and absorbed the pain people were experiencing. Families of four or five would cram onto the back of a two-person Vespa, and many children were without the protection of a helmet. Many of the markets were unsanitary, the streets were crowded with people just sitting on the side of the road, and hygiene was obviously neglected. My stomach twisted in distress.

The looks in their eyes spoke to my soul as I energetically experienced their reality. Something was shifting inside me as certain scenes threatened to haunt me eternally. The child without legs who was struggling to use a skateboard to be mobile was now a vivid and permanent memory.

I ached for more people to see what we were witnessing. The energy was mind boggling. I kept gasping to catch my breath, often wondering if I was going to collapse. I hid most of the impact Vietnam was having on me; it was too overwhelming to express.

Vietnam was having an effect on me in a way prior travel had not. This trip was moving slower, in a more natural flow. The colors were vibrant. The scenes were so dramatic. My senses were working in overdrive, and my mind was recording everything like a video camera.

A few days later, Jamie arranged for us to each have a session with her Reiki healer whom she raved about. *It's really wild that two energy readers have entered my life in just a matter of weeks, and never once before. Talk about perfect timing.*

Her home was the definition of tranquil. An instant Zen feeling swept over me, and she simply placed her hands on my forehead. Within a split second, a forceful shift in energy demanded my attention as her hands began to heat up. *Whoa, what is this?* She told me the same things Dawn, the psychic, had said: I was going to help a lot of people, and there was trapped pain from a guy. *Apparently there's no hiding that one. Well, that sounds familiar. I want to help people, but how? Ahh, what in the world is my purpose?*

As her hands grew warmer, the sensation was like something being ripped out of me. She then moved around to my side and put her hands on my stomach. There was a commanding pull on my right side, as if something was trying to escape. It was almost painful. Then a few tears just silently trailed down my cheeks without my consent, control, or even conscious thought.

Prior to the trip, I had neglected the healing process and instead had buried the pain. As unhealthy as it was, the tears from the heartbreak a few weeks prior were still trapped within. I don't think I wanted to admit that it was real or that I had been so foolish. The shock hadn't budged. The desire to erase him continued to grow.

So many specific personal things were mentioned, many of which involved my family and friends. The healer even explained that I had a very strong pull to Asia and that my energy did not match that of the United States—eventually, I would have to leave.

She also told me that I had more healing power than anyone she had ever met and that I would be traveling around helping people with it. She told me I was on the right path but that I was unclear about what it was. *Yes, I have no idea where this is going. How can I heal people? I'm so confused and overwhelmed. What is happening?* It was a disorienting experience, and my emotions were completely stirred up.

Afterward, I went out by the pool and curled up on the healer's shaded lawn furniture to write what she had just said to me. The stillness of everything brought awareness to each and every blink. It was all in slow motion. There was no such thing as time. There was no technology. There were no distractions. I was allowed to just simply be. It was freedom. *What a special place, thank you!*

Giving into the inviting water, the trapped tears finally escaped my guarded wall of denial. A few moments of soundless sobbing left a sense of lightness in my body. The healing power of that backyard shined a new light of perspective, revealing a heightened plateau of awareness.

Through the flood of gratitude, I noticed that Vietnamese music was playing softly, a woman was singing beautifully in the distance, the birds were chirping, a butterfly was circling me, and I was hypnotized by the bright reflections of the sun that were dancing on the pool. *How am I here? This is flawless.*

Finally seeing clearly, each and every flower was appreciated, such perfection acknowledged. I felt inner expansion at a perplexing speed. My soul was on a journey, and I just had to keep up. It was my time to seek the truth and to meet every crevice of this wild spirit. *Wow, I feel so alive, so insanely alive. What's happening to me? Where is this going?*

As we explored Vietnam, my gut gently, and repeatedly, whispered that it wasn't time to attempt meditation yet. There was no need to argue; it would feel right when it was time. I was too wrapped up in the moment to overthink it. Little did I know that the most life-changing thing I had ever experienced was about to happen—everything was about to change—in Thailand.

16

WELCOME TO THAILAND

We started the day in Vietnam, spent the afternoon in Singapore, and were now at a resort in Phuket, Thailand, which we had booked just two days before.

The cab pulled up to a resort tucked away into a hillside by the beach. It was dark out, so we couldn't possibly grasp the full beauty of where we were staying, but the morning guaranteed breathtaking views.

After checking in, we grabbed dinner at the resort restaurant. Because it was so late, we were the only people there. I closed my eyes for a second and focused on the sounds of the ocean and the caress of the warm breeze. Then the song "Here in Heaven" started playing through the speakers. *There's that song again—wow, I never hear that song—interesting timing again.*

The next morning, I blasted out of bed in hyper mode. I yanked the curtains open, and the ocean was exposed in unprecedented color. It was too perfect to be real, but there we were. The view from our oversized balcony consisted of scattered islands, richly colored flowers, and crashing green waves. The potential for an epic day was obvious. *I love life, and I love Thailand!*

I *was* in heaven as I sank my feet into the sand and got lost in the 3-D postcard I had apparently stepped into. We instantly wished we were staying longer than a few days and realized that the beaches were more entrancing than we could have imagined. *Thank you for this priceless moment.*

The water was so salty that we just floated effortlessly. Each wave seemed to be systematically washing away my pain—a welcomed healing process. I had surrendered. Looking up, I noticed a small cliff of rocks along the side of our hotel.

"Meditate there."

Yeah, that feels right. Cool. It wasn't time to do this yet, though. Instead, it was time to explore. The next few days consisted of riding four-wheelers through the dramatic terrain, enjoying massages on the beach, reading by the pool, riding elephants, and simply indulging in authentic Thai food. *Ahh, I'm at peace.*

Our room had a copy of *The Teachings of Buddha*, so it seemed obvious that this was a fitting read for the beach. Within a couple days, I raced through it.

Some of my jotted-down quotes included, "There is nothing in this world that is not mind-created," "The mind is the master of every situation," and "Human beings move in the direction of their thoughts." These were the same messages from *The Secret* and from studying the wisest teachers, leaders, and philosophers. *Okay, this is obviously the right path. It's oozing truth. Hmm, imagine if we applied this truth. Imagine if we worked together. Imagine our potential. Imagine if we stopped living in fear and chose love?*

There was a reference to fame and praise being similar to

incense, as they are nice for a while but inevitably disappear. In full agreement, it was difficult to stop thinking about the damaging effects of the media. *It's all an illusion—one that hurts so many people. Why are we still falling for this? Women are so objectified, and it causes so many body-image and self-worth issues. Why is everything so obviously designed to make us fight, compete, feel inadequate, and choose a side? Why are we allowing this policy of divide and conquer to continue?*

It reinforced how powerful the mind is and how plausible peace within and among us is. Reading that enlightenment means that one is free from the control of foolish delusions resonated deeply. It was fascinating to read about the battle of the ego and the soul, as well as the potential for true peace.

Intentions were quickly set to reach that level of consciousness in my lifetime—although I was completely clueless as to how this would happen. Of course, this was not a self-declaration to any religious affiliation, just an acknowledgment of some very obvious truth, truth that unites us with logic and love.

My imagination zipped off to my vision of our world's potential, imagining the benefits of embracing a more compassionate nature. *Well, this trip is obviously heading in a stronger spiritual direction than anticipated, and I'm totally open to that!*

The last evening was euphoric as the soothing breeze made for a comfortable state of being. After a drawn-out dinner, we went to the beach and ventured out on the still water with some of the hotel rafts—not that we were supposed to be using them that late.

We were the only people out there and, in the distance, lightning bolts danced harmlessly on the horizon, causing dramatic shades of purple to illuminate the sky. It was our own private light show. We didn't have a care in the world; it was too surreal to grasp. Each breath was appreciated, every wave soothing my shattered heart.

We then saw someone on shore shining a flashlight around and thought that we had been caught with the rafts, so we frantically paddled ourselves in and started wrestling the harsh waves near the shore. We darted toward the hotel with, of course, no one chasing after us. Adrenaline and laughter took over.

"It's time to meditate."

What? Now? But it's dark out, and I'm ready for bed! It was our last night there, so the instruction to meditate was surprising. Not thinking too much about it, we decided to change and try meditating for a while. It was an odd shift in activities, but the feeling was only getting stronger.

It was impossible to not notice how peaceful the evening was as we each climbed onto our own platforms. Karin was angled toward the beach on a lower level of rocks with her back to me. My positioning was facing out toward the still water. There wasn't a sound to be heard. *This is absolute perfection. Okay, let's give this meditation thing a shot.*

I settled into a comfortable pose with straightened posture and focused on breathing deeply. Other than studying some techniques, meditation was still a new concept. So I closed my eyes, relaxed, and let go.

Well, that was until I was interrupted. Just as I was starting to center myself, *someone* began pushing on the front of my shoulders, trying to force me backward. My eyes ripped open in sheer shock.

There was no one there. Karin was still down below on a lower level of rocks—completely still with her back to me. I shook my head and decided to ignore it, writing it off as a really strong gust of wind (despite the supreme stillness). Completely confused, my eyes reclosed in search of that former state of mind. *That was really weird.*

Within just a few seconds, it happened again, only with more force. This time, it shoved me backward so hard I had to put my hands behind my back to push myself up. That's all it took to officially freak me out. *Whoa, what is this?*

Panic set in. My racing thoughts accelerated congruently with an exaggerated heart rate. Flushed with shock—and uncontrollable curiosity—my head continued to shake in disbelief. *This doesn't make any sense. What is this? Seriously, what in the world is this?*

With closed eyes, the same force pushed on my shoulders, sending me flopping back almost completely on my back. Mind you, my legs were still crossed Indian-style, so it was very uncomfortable, and I just barely caught myself.

This time, the intensity was revved up even more, and my head flopped to the left to see if this was happening to Karin. It wasn't. However, she was now looking at me.

The awkwardness of the current position was apparent, but my silent tears were unseen in the dark. Terrified and gasping for breath, my head swirled with chaos. *Whoa! Whoa! Whoa! What is this?*

The words didn't exist in my vocabulary, or yelling out to her would have been my instinct. There was a mysterious silence in the air, as if I would have been scolded for speaking. Instead, remaining quiet, completely baffled and in sheer shock, was all I could do.

It let up, allowing me to bounce back into an upright position. Just as the thought that it was over crossed my mind, a force blasted me back so strongly, my whole being started sobbing and shaking—without so much as a whisper of noise. My arms didn't have time to react as my body folded into a rather painful position.

Now completely pinned down, flat on my back, the rocks behind me were digging in deeply. This was obviously not a position to consciously choose to be in. *How is this happening?*

As uncomfortable as it was, I could have stayed there all night soaking in the energy around and within me and releasing my pain. The pressure was released, and my weary body went springing forward, and I scrambled to grasp some comprehension of what had just happened. The magnificence of it all began to race through me.

There was no sense of time. There was no sense of anything. I was just spinning. *Whoa! Whoa! Whoa! What just happened?*

So there I was, back to my original position, frozen in shock. Then out of the gentle water, there was an explosive splash against the rocks, as if it were a stern warning. It was the only wave that crashed on the rocks the whole time we were there, only amplifying the throbbing in my head.

One glance at Karin, and my blown mind was apparent to her. In the years we had been friends, she had almost never seen me cry. This was the first time she had ever seen me sob in a way that seemed to come from nowhere and for no apparent reason. We had just been laughing shortly before the unexpected wrestling match with my invisible opponent.

We climbed off the rocks and started walking back to the resort in silence. My eyes were completely bugged out of my head, and the tears only picked up speed in an illogical way. The faucet had finally been turned on. My chest heaved up and down as I tried to catch my breath and stop the trembling.

Of course, at this time, the awareness of how crazy this all sounded occurred to me momentarily. That thought was quickly overpowered though. Somehow nothing and everything made sense to me simultaneously. *That was so powerful! What does this mean? Why did this happen? Will it happen again? How will anyone ever understand this? Will I?*

17

BACK TO REALITY

The next morning, my eyes sprang open, and every cell in my body eagerly raced to make sure it wasn't all a dream. My eyelids were puffed up and crusted together from crying. My mind was still blown, of course.

Once we began to travel back to Vietnam, we realized just how out of it we were. A newfound energy coursed through me. It was a weightlessness and warmth unlike anything I had ever experienced. It was a state that I wished would remain preserved.

However, Karin was having the polar opposite experience. She could barely keep her eyes open, and she kept saying, "I feel like I'm dead." It was as though she had vanished. It reminded me of that day in the park with my mom, when I was nothing more than an empty shell—only more extreme.

There was no explaining this to anyone for a while, at least not until I processed it myself. My mind rushed for answers. *What am I supposed to do with this?*

Just before we left, we had a long layover in South Korea, so we took the train into Seoul and spent some time strolling around. We had become accustomed to the tropical weather and were not prepared for the freezing temperatures, but we still made it memorable. Then it was good-bye to the surreal life I had been borrowing for the last few weeks. *Good-bye, my dear Asia, I will miss you deeply!*

As soon as I arrived in Sonoma, my stomach started to ache. This was partly because it was overwhelming to think about what to do with my life now, but it was mostly due to the fact that I couldn't wrap my mind around what had happened in Thailand. It was also because I had picked up some mysterious illness from my trip.

Asia had triggered an even deeper burning desire to help people. With no clue as to how to make that happen, my head just flopped back in a defeated manner as I begged for some guidance. *What are my next steps? I've returned to absolute uncertainty. Thank you for guiding me toward my dreams. Thank you for my inner circle being able to join forces with me on a humanity mission. Thank you for the ability to make people's dreams come true. Thank you for freedom!*

Now returning to speed America, it became evident how liberating a month away from my phone had been. *We are suffering so much because of the conditioning. Where is this technology going? Why are we so distracted from our basic human nature? Why are we turning into robots? Why are we dumbing down our language? It seems like we are devolving. I liked people better before we hid behind screens.*

"Check your Facebook."

Huh? Facebook? Yuck. No thanks. I hadn't looked at that for a month either, and I couldn't think of a reason to. *What am I supposed to do next in my life?*

"Check your Facebook."

Well, it's not like I'm pressed for time. Sure enough, there was a message from my friend Nick asking me to meet up with him and another friend because they wanted to talk to me about something. *That's random.*

"Go see Nick."

With my weakened body, the last thing that sounded appealing was socializing. Naturally, my gut held a newfound power over me—I was scared to not listen to it. *Aye aye, Universe!*

Upon seeing the guys, it was easy to notice that they had both lost weight and were more energetic than usual. They burst into a passionate rant about a natural product they'd been taking. Both of them had started using it a few months prior and raved about the effects.

They explained that they were working collaboratively with a team, including the owners of the company, and they were asking their friends and family to do a trial month of the product. There was even a guarantee of a full refund if anyone wasn't satisfied. They had never talked about anything remotely like this before.

My gut was encouraging me, and I figured there wasn't any risk in trying a natural product for a month. *Is this how I am supposed to help people? It's ironic that it came in just an hour and a half before heading back to New York, after traveling for a month. Interesting timing.*

18

IN MY CAVE

The trial experiment with the health product remained private with a few other people. Surprisingly, after just a few weeks, all of us were feeling a variety of results, and my intrigue grew. *Well, this is random. Guess that's the theme of my life now.*

Being open to everything was exhilarating, as the latest vision boards were fueled with gratitude and faith. Basically, my chronic daydreaming was now guided by purposeful techniques. Everything slowed down, despite my eagerness. I was shedding more layers and learning so much about the depths of my soul. *Wow, it's so nice to have time to sort out my mind and understand myself more.*

Before heading back out for another adventure, one of the swirling books within me had to be yanked out. The easiest one was a short book to help nice guys with dating, so night after night this was my entire life—up to fifteen hours a day. Locked up tight in the writing cave, my mind was finally being trained to structure and organize a book.

Outside of my family, my social life was on pause. External negativity, drama, and distractions were blocked out as the sole focus was on exploring my mind and inner self. I just needed a break from the world.

My time was in my control. No rules, no obligations, no schedule—just constant introspection and rapid personal growth. The "pause" button in life had been hit, and thinking freely was addictive. *Wow, this is kind of what retirement feels like. I'm so happy I didn't wait decades to see life from this vantage point. I see why older people tell us to do things when we are young, as there are no guarantees.*

Just before Christmas, the seventy-page book was finished, and I hoped to sell it as an e-book. I figured this would be the first possible source of passive income for me. With a taste of the writer's high, I was hungry for more.

However, my gut demanded that I put it to the side for the time being. It was very anticlimactic, but completing a writing piece of that length had built my confidence to tackle *the* book—the mysterious book that had tormented me for most of my life.

Other than my huge stack of scattered ideas, notes, and random paragraphs, there was no structure to the book yet. It wasn't for lack of trying, though. It just remained brutally blocked. I was still tortured by its nagging presence. *What can I write that's different? How can I uniquely inspire people? How can I teach in an original way? How can I untangle these polarized ideas? What in the world is my purpose, and how can I fulfill it if I don't know what to write about?*

The product seemed like a healthy direction. On one of the conference calls, I was told that the owners were going to visit Sonoma, so the team I was working with wanted me to be there. It seemed like the obvious next step, and any excuse to go to Sonoma was fine by me.

19

IT'S TIME FOR A WIN

A one-way ticket to San Francisco launched me straight into instant networking. There was a heated energy pulling me forward, and I was feeling great about all of it—that is, until I was asked to get up and speak at the upcoming presentation. We had set it up for the local community, and some of my friends and the owners of the company were going to be there. My instinct was to bolt in the other direction. *Oh, no! No, no, no.*

"*Do it.*"

Ahh, no way! Public speaking has always been my biggest fear. The accumulated energy of the audience gets me all worked up. Then the overheating begins, my knees start shaking, and anxiety plagues my sweaty body—yet death doesn't trigger a physical reaction.

"*Do it.*"

Really? Please, no! Uhh, fine! Damn it, gut! I reluctantly agreed because I knew I wasn't getting out of this one. It was a fear that needed to be faced. Period.

Thankfully, there was a distraction—New Year's Eve. As Karin and I were deciding what to do, I heard a familiar voice say, *"Go to Napa."* Karin had originally wanted to go to San Francisco to meet up with some people but ended up opting for a more mellow evening in wine country with me.

By the time we arrived in Napa, we were extremely hungry. We had rented a room and took a cab to the downtown area. We went to a few restaurants, and each one had literally just closed. All of them recommended that we go to Morimoto, our favorite local sushi restaurant. *Okay, that seems like where we're supposed to be.*

When we got there, we sat down to get some food in the small dining section they had left open in the front. Just as we let out a sigh of relief, the waitress came back over and apologized for the misunderstanding. The kitchen was closed, so this meant no food—anywhere.

We sat there, frustrated for a minute, and then the gentleman next to us explained that he had ordered a bunch of sushi for his friends who weren't showing up now, so it was going to be wasted.

The waitress confirmed what he was saying, and we slid over for some sushi. We had no intention of staying longer, but we were informed there was a party in the back. It seemed as if we were supposed to be there, and the music started to yank us in.

Just as we were about to walk in, one of the girls at the door recognized my friend, and we stopped to say hello. After talking for a few moments, she asked us if we had filled out an entry for the drawing, which we had not. We hadn't even noticed it.

So we filled out our names and didn't even think to ask what it was for.

"You just won that."

I reactively blurted out, "We totally just won that." Karin just smirked and didn't respond. I still hadn't inquired what it was for—I assumed a gift certificate for the restaurant or something comparable. *Sweet, I love sushi!*

My attention was on the fact that my body had started to dance to the music in the distance. As we started to dance, a young guy came up to me to initiate conversation and ask if he could join.

I prefer to dance alone, so I stopped dancing to talk to him. In no time we were chatting about confidence, nonverbal communication, and how to build attraction. It was fun helping nice guys feel more assured in their skills to approach women. Although it still didn't feel like it was my dream career path for some reason. I sensed something else but couldn't see it clearly yet.

It was incredibly loud in there, and we were both wrapped up in our teaching moment, so I didn't notice Karin yelling my name. She was saying, "They're calling you. They're calling you." Sure enough, the DJ was giving the final call for my name. *I guess I just won that little gift certificate. That's cool.*

When the prize was announced, I realized this was more than a gift certificate for sushi. Instead, it was a romantic package for two in Maui at a five-star Asian-inspired resort—including spa packages. *Seriously? An Asian-inspired trip right after going to Asia?*

What was additionally shocking was that an image of Maui, Hawaii, was on my vision board. Not another island—that exact one. *Are you kidding me? Thank you, Universe! Wow! I'm obsessed with the Law of Attraction. This is ridiculously fun!*

It had been the most random series of incidents that had guided us to be in that exact place at the exact time to win that prize. It was also because I was in town to meet the owners of the health product that this had happened. *Well, okay then. Happy New Year!*

When the owners of the health product got to town, we hit it off extremely well, and before I knew it, I had somehow been invited to private business dinners and meetings with the family and other professionals—just like I had visualized.

Of course, speaking publicly wasn't as bad as I had anticipated—although my nervousness was clearly evident. I appreciated the opportunity to face my fear.

That evening, a few of us had been invited to go out to eat with the owners, and at one point I made a reference to the Law of Attraction. I noticed that the guy next to me had perked up with interest. We started talking and continued to do so most of the evening about how it works and our experiences with it.

He told me that he worked with someone from the movie *The Secret*. He also mentioned that he could introduce me to other powers of influence, including Oprah. This was all beginning to feel completely detached from reality. *Whoa! What is going on? Is this real?*

My schedule was determined in the moment, depending on the situations and people coming in. So when the owners of the product invited me to Vegas for a conference, it was obviously the next step. *Where is this whirlwind leading?*

So I zipped over to Vegas for a few days to learn more. Listening to speakers share countless tears, heartbreaking stories, and authentic gratitude for this transformative product was so inspiring. The product was clearly changing people's lives dramatically.

The doctor in Sonoma had invited me to another Vegas conference in March and told me that he could set me up with a mentor who was an expert in the Law of Attraction. Everything was moving so fast. I didn't know if that was good or not—it just was.

GAME TIME

Now back in New York, I attempted to process my juggling-act lifestyle. *It's finally time to relax.*

"It's time to read The Game.*"*

No, thank you. Not now. Sorry, I'm too tired. I had purchased the book a couple months prior but had been wrapped up with the chaos of everything else. I was thoroughly enjoying the comfort of my pajamas—so much so that I had decided to spend the day in them. A break was necessary.

All the networking had depleted every drop of energy I had left in me. The plan was to take a full, uneventful day off. I had been "on" for a month straight and had burned the candle at both ends, like always.

"It's time to read The Game.*"*

I said no thank you! Shh, quiet, gut! I was basking in the idea of doing absolutely nothing. I needed to recharge.

The downtime with my family was much appreciated and necessary. Sadly, they had been a witness to my torturous loss of appetite since my trip to Asia. I was in a fog and would unintentionally go up to five days without food. It was the only time I've ever struggled to eat.

There was an undeniable change in my personality as I desperately scrambled to make sense of the inner—and therefore, outer—confusion of my life. I didn't recognize myself; my frustrated, desperate energy was even turning me off. That trip had impacted me more than I was aware of. Something was wrong, but I couldn't explain it.

Now at the point of a crazy roller coaster ride where it slows down before it drops back into unpredictable motion, my stomach was doing flips in anticipation. I didn't know the next steps, other than going to Vegas—but that was a couple of months away. *What am I supposed to do next? Please give me guidance! Can you please just spell it out for me?*

"It's time to read The Game.*"*

Oh, wow, are you kidding me? I sprang up in a moment of annoyance, went upstairs, and reluctantly grabbed the book. I then stomped back downstairs and plopped on the couch again. *Fine, I will read* The Game!

I couldn't help but wonder why this had to be done at this exact moment. *Why this book? Don't I ever get a break from all this?*

The pickup-artist community had continued to come up in conversations when I was in L.A., and I didn't know how this was going to factor into chasing my dreams. There was a strong instinctual pull toward this world, and I knew it was going to lead me closer to my dreams if I listened.

So I obediently settled onto the couch and started my "homework." Within a few chapters, however, I became wildly impressed with Neil's writing style and bluntness.

My gut then gave me an unprecedented command. I was instructed to contact a specific man in the book. *Huh? How? More importantly, why?*

Never before had there been an urge to reach out to a person in a book. I wasn't exactly impressed by the individual that I was being encouraged to contact—in fact, he made my face scrunch up with resistance. *This is silly. I don't get it. Seriously, why him? Why not Neil? He is someone that I would like to meet!*

As I was questioning this simple request, the next instruction was provided: *"Reach out to this individual on his social media."* So that's what I did. I was clueless as to what I was actually expecting to accomplish.

However, he instantly responded and started recommending reading materials. We then spoke on the phone about the power of the mind, and he mentioned possibly mentoring me. *What does he have to do with all this?*

To my surprise, he then asked me if I wanted to go to a radio show in Malibu next month—at Neil's house. He was scheduled to be a guest on the show. Of course, I agreed. *Wow! I guess I am supposed to meet Neil. Thank you!*

How had I just picked up a book and been invited to the author's house by the end of the day—all while in my pajamas? *Law of Attraction, you're making my stomach do flips!*

After a couple of weeks of recuperation, continual research, and passionate visualizing, I was ready for the next round of adventure. So I booked a one-way ticket and was off, with no idea when I would be back. *Here we go, another round. Why L.A., though? I never feel like myself there. What does the world's top pickup artist possibly have to do with this?*

21

CERTAINLY UNCERTAIN

Chicago was the first stop, and a few more friends signed up to do the trial experiment. Being in constant motion and working collaboratively with a team had become addictive. I was hungry for more. I was acknowledged as one of the top new salespeople in the company, and that just fired me up more. *All I want is for my favorite people to be released from work obligations so that we can be free to work on creative philanthropy and travel the world.*

I'm sure my lifestyle looked fun on the outside, but I was being tormented on the inside at an unprecedented level. My sincere intentions were inevitably misperceived. I couldn't explain what was happening, because I didn't get it.

While focusing on the business, I was also anxiously awaiting the radio show. I had absolutely no idea what to expect. There were so many questions. I had butterflies about all of it.

I had set a time to meet up with the possible new "mentor,"

who lived in the same area as my friend Jessica. What I wasn't expecting was that he lived right across the street from her, literally just a matter of feet away. *What are the chances of that, considering how large L.A. is? Seriously. How convenient...and weird.* It was almost suspiciously orchestrated.

SHOW TIME

The drive along the coast to Malibu only partially calmed my nerves as I gazed at the vastness of the ocean. Unfortunately, my anxiety had apparently hopped in the car as an uninvited passenger. The heat was racing for my face. *Ahh, go away! You're the worst! Great, I'm sweating and fidgeting—very attractive. Why do I have to be so socially awkward?*

When I got inside, I was completely misplaced as everyone scurried around in preparation. I took a seat and then a woman sat down next to me. She turned to me and within moments asked, "Do you believe in the Law of Attraction?"

It was incredible how many people blurted out those words now, yet never did before. We talked passionately about how we had ended up in Malibu at a radio show through the power of attraction. We then exchanged contact information and continued to chat.

I was simply supposed to be there, at that exact moment, in that exact seat, exchanging that exact number. I could feel it. I knew it. I just didn't know why. *We have a strong past-life connection. She also has something to do with my dreams, but what? The scavenger hunt continues; thanks for another clue.*

The show was an absolute blast, and there were no shortages of characters. I appreciated how Neil didn't hold back from speaking his mind or getting to the truth.

Then it happened. As I was watching from the peanut gallery, Neil turned to the audience to ask each of us a question. Being put on the spot like that caused instant panic. It was high school all over again.

My hand slowly stretched open as Neil handed me the microphone. To my surprise, a rush of adrenaline took over like never before. Everything slowed down and I was able to compose myself enough to answer his questions. In fact, I was having fun. It was so energizing. *Why does this feel so natural?*

He was far too busy to have time to talk to me for more than a moment, but I carried the rush of being pushed out of my comfort zone for quite some time. He had unknowingly pushed me forward, and I couldn't believe how much I wanted to do it again. *Okay, how do I achieve what he has?*

23

SMILE FOR THE CAMERA

Unfortunately when I returned home, something strange happened with my dog, Newman. It was about three in the morning and I was still up dancing. He started behaving in a way that he never had. Out of a dead sleep, he walked by me and was interacting with *someone* that wasn't there. I swear he was smiling.

His tale was wagging ferociously, and he was looking up at something and softly whimpering. The energy was thick. I instinctually teared up and hugged him. I told him to hang on as long as he could. *That was intense. Why did that feel like a calling to the other side? Am I being paranoid?*

As soon as my feet hit the airport floor, I was off; the social buzz was waiting on cue. There were seven thousand people there, and the audience was generating a force field of upbeat and youthful energy.

The motivational speakers were absolutely mind blowing, especially because of their dramatic stories of near-death experiences, mental illness, trauma, being broke, deep struggles, losing their minds, times of desperation, bad decisions, and many other stories that I didn't have, at least not at their caliber. *How will people relate to me? It's the deep pain and extreme mistakes that seem to be the greatest asset. Ahh, how can I do this? I know that's where I belong, but with my skin issues and anxiety, I can't do this.*

As I was sitting there during an intermission, I decided to call my family—a decision that was instantly regretted. My dad's voice gave it away, and my body tensed in a protective response as a lump took my throat hostage.

He informed me that Newman had cancer and was either going to need his leg amputated or would need to be put down. I couldn't breathe. *No, not Newman.*

The room started to spin as the thick chatter swirled around me. Everything slowed down as the surrounding happy circus continued, but the only sound was the thumping of my heart. I had been hoping that my feeling was wrong. I should have known better. It wasn't the first time I had sensed death.

Then there was a sudden announcement that the entire event was going to turn into a scene for a movie. Out of nowhere, bright lights came on, a camera crew appeared, an actress walked out on stage, and they started filming. *Seriously? Now?*

When the scene was finished, the entire place cleared out as everyone dashed out the door, but I remained. Then the actress came back out on stage to shoot a scene without the crowd being present. So it was just the two of us, and the camera crew, while she read a speech.

With a blank stare and a motionless body, I listened as she read the same lines over and over. It seemed as though she were saying it specifically for my soul, as the messages from the Universe were transparent.

She kept repeating, "If there's one thing I know for sure, it's that life can change in a heartbeat, and even with that gift of vision, you can get knocked down and never see it coming. And there's not a lot of cushion on that floor. Then it all comes down to faith. Believing makes it possible. Faith makes it real."

The exaggerated screams from the lobby left me wondering how I was going to coexist with this hyper sea of humans. I desperately wanted to leave, but there were obligations booked in California. Denial took over. *I feel so trapped.*

24

RUNNING ON EMPTY

Dream chasing had taken its toll and had left me with a heavy cloak of doubt. My empty self was just going through the motions. *How do I not have anything to show for my efforts? Why is this so painful? Why am I a million miles from my dreams? I'm so tired. What the hell is my purpose?* The search party for answers doubled in force. I was spiraling even farther down into my cave. *I just want to be alone.*

I didn't know where to settle down, or if I was even supposed to do that. My next steps were blurred and confusing. The writing was blocked, and I remained clueless about how to put myself out there. I was meeting people at such a fast rate that it felt like everyone was just zipping by in a blurred flash—similar to a dream state. It was impossible to recharge. I was just a ghost watching the scenes flying by.

Simultaneously, I was completely devastated as I watched everything unravel with the health product business. The momentum had evaporated. It seemed to happen almost overnight. It was an expensive product, and people were struggling to sell it. By no fault of their own, my friends also didn't have the same opportunities to truly grasp the complex science of the product or the profound impact it had on so many lives. My heart was breaking faster than I could process.

$$\Diamond$$

A few days later, I was able to escape to the ocean for sunrise, begging for answers. The journey was testing and challenging me, and I didn't know if I was passing or failing. As I asked for help, two rocks, one white and one black, washed up to my feet, and my instinct was to scoop them up and keep them with me.

At that exact moment, I thought about Zach's story. I remembered how he had told me that things became unbearably difficult, but he didn't give up, even when he wanted to. *I don't know how to do this, though. I'm just spinning in circles. My life is falling apart in an effort to create my dream life. Everything is distorted. I don't feel like myself. It's like something else is controlling my life.*

The next morning, I went to see someone who was about to pass away. It had been a while since I had seen him, but my gut had told me to say good-bye. It was certainly not an easy task, especially considering my emotional depletion. He had always been good to me, so I knew this would mean a lot to him.

Tim and I had very intellectual conversations over the years, and he had been a positive influence in my life. We shared a passion for learning and reading. We would talk for hours over dinner about life and literature, while I soaked in his wisdom. Surprisingly, seeing him gave me an unexpected source of strength and perspective that I truly needed at that moment. It was a flash of light that lit up the dark place I was in. It was good-bye to a true teacher.

25

UNEXPECTED AUDITION

Despite the extreme socializing, it was an isolating reality, and I ached for my former sense of security and routine. I was moving too fast to get involved with anyone emotionally, and therefore, physically, so I was lonely. Eating and sleeping at this point had become alarmingly forced. The stress and disappointments were just destroying me. I was the walking dead.

Then at the last minute, Neil's sound guy contacted Stephanie to get my contact information. We had met briefly at the first show, and now he was calling me to offer to pick me up if I were able to go to the show. It was just a matter of getting the green light from Neil because only a few people could attend.

The suspense was killing me. It was baffling how strongly I wanted the chance to just sit on the sidelines of a radio show. That environment had triggered something primal in me.

At that moment, Zach's story popped into my head again,

and I thought about how he had done anything to just sit in the back of the room, watching people do what he loved. Finding strength in his story, his courage was continuing to rev my drive. *Just keep going. It's going to pay off. Don't give up!*

With no time to spare, the green light was given. On the drive over, Neil's sound guy told me that he had been casting for a month for a radio show and wanted to know if I would be interested in auditioning. *Really? Me?*

He then introduced the radio host to me on speakerphone and set up a meeting for the following morning, which was perfect because my flight was leaving just hours later. It was another open door—and just in the nick of time. Even with a flicker of hope, I was clearly out of it at the radio show. My heart was grieving the loss of Newman, as he had just been put down.

The next morning was a heavy blur. However, when the host walked into the recording studio, her presence was sweet and infectious, the connection instant. Her life experiences, temperament, and charisma were unlike any other woman I had ever met. Her positive energy was bringing me back to life. *What an unexpected source of strength.*

She was wildly supportive, and our energy was unbelievably compatible. We taped a test run show, and I was sold. We both had matching passions and a desire to help and inspire women. We exchanged stories of our adventures, and she even brought up the Law of Attraction. The heat inside assured me this was the right track. Neil's radio shows were pushing me to build confidence and face my social anxiety disorder head on.

They decided I was a fit. I had a reason to move out to California with no time to spare. *Am I going to be able to speak my truths like Neil?*

26

THE TRUTH HURTS

Over the next few weeks, I packed my car and prepared for the move. During this time, the block that had tormented me for the majority of my life was magically released. It was as though a veil had finally been lifted. Just like that, the writing started to flow. Clarity washed over me as the fire within me lit my fears up like gasoline on wood. *Wow, I can't believe this! It's finally happening.*

My "radio script" notes were now morphing into a book. Fierce momentum surged through me. I was again writing up to fifteen hours a day, seven days a week. I was teaching the lessons that I had learned and placing my stories throughout. I was sprinting toward that finish line.

My gut was demanding that I go see Dawn. So I went to see her and quickly realized that what she was saying, I didn't want to hear—but needed to. She told me that I was going out to

California for a different reason than I thought. She told me that I would be given more spiritual things and psychic things. *Huh? What in the world does that mean?*

She informed me that I was not ready for what I was hoping would happen and that this was all about timing. She also explained that what I was trying to manifest was not the best option for me at that time and instructed me to keep it more open. She said I was in a vortex, very scattered and way too static. *Yeah, that's for sure. How do I change that? Now I'm even more confused.*

Dawn predicted that I was going to be moving around a lot in a new area of California and that I would have a lower spinal injury. She then said I would be moving back to wine country and described a white house with black shutters in Napa. I had never wanted to live there, so that was hard to believe.

There was a prediction that I would only be living there for a few months and that a guy with a huge heart was going to sweep me off my feet at that time. Her eyes lit up in a way I'd never seen before as she explained that the connection between us was going to be ten million times stronger than anything I have ever experienced.

She said he was great at painting, that he would become my business partner, and that we would be traveling and helping lots of people—basically that he was my dream guy and would help make my dreams come true. He was the guy I had sensed and talked about most of my life.

The next prediction was that after Napa, I would move toward San Jose and have a quiet place near the ocean to finish the book. She said I would also take energy classes and start healing people.

She explained that I would be in a position of management and leadership, in charge of a lot of people, and that what I was going to get involved in was going to be huge, and that I had to make sure that I kept control of it. She told me there would be a camera crew and to not let them put makeup on me. The book came up again, and she said it would be as big as I think. She also predicted that I would win money and kept mentioning poetry.

The energy in the room was out of this world, and I ached for all of that to be true—except the spinal injury, of course. I too had tapped into that energy frequency she was feeling and never wanted to leave. My heart exploded with desire for that to be my reality. It sounded rather far-fetched, but my gut was screaming that it was all going to happen.

As much as I wanted to work with the other host, my gut was assuring me that to move forward, I had to work alone. As disappointing as it was, I had to assume that there was a reason for it. There seemed to be another plan in place. *Maybe I'm not ready. In fact, I know I'm not.*

The word *alone* was haunting me, always alone. My personal journey of unforeseen twists, turns, disappointments, and hard-learned lessons continued to leave me in a state of isolating pain. I just wasn't ready to put myself out there, and the book needed to be unscrambled. The confidence wasn't there, and Dawn's predictions matched my recent gut feelings.

It did occur to me that it was that exact experience that gave me the courage to pack up my car, commit to moving, and crank out half of a book at lightning speed. It had also lifted my spirits when I was in a very painful place. Each experience was leading to the next, teaching me lessons and giving me just enough hope to continue.

Impatience was inevitable because I could see and feel what was up ahead. I just didn't know how to reach it. There were so many people and places that were mentioned before the most desired predictions came into play. The suspense was creating unbearable anxiety. *This scavenger hunt is so confusing! Please help me to decode this puzzle! I have to see the final picture. Please spare my sanity!*

27

A DASH OF ALCHEMY

All in all, it seemed like I was back at square one. Now even more perplexed and heartbroken, I admitted to myself how lost I was. It was like walking around a maze in the dark, with a blindfold on, kind of lost. *Ahh, I want my life back. What is all of this? Where is this leading? I just want out of this tornado! No one understands me at this point, and this is hurting the people I love.*

Unfortunately my family continued to be dragged on the roller coaster with me. Up and down, elated then crushed. Hopeful and then disappointed. My heart was breaking even more because of that sad reality—in fact, it was killing me. *Seriously, what now? I can't take much more.*

"*Read* The Alchemist.*"*

Huh? Now? My sister and her boyfriend had repeatedly encouraged me to read this book recently. In fact, they were adamant about it, despite never having recommended a book to me before. *Maybe later.*

"Read The Alchemist.*"*

I was so discouraged about everything that I decided it couldn't hurt to start it. I sank into the couch, and to my surprise, I didn't put the book down until the last word was read. The whole story resonated with me as I found strength in reading about the soul's purpose and overcoming challenges. The main character even went across the desert, which oddly motivated me to have the courage to drive across the country alone.

Then I reached the part of the story when the main character picks up a white-and-black stone. I quickly flashed back to the morning that I had instinctually picked up the white and black rocks that washed up to me. I had been carrying them in my purse ever since. *What a very strange coincidence. This is a powerful little book. As crazy as this all is, it's obviously my soul's path. It's remarkable how much I feel led by books at the exact moment I need a message. What was Dawn talking about with the psychic and spiritual things? What could that mean?*

This was officially the most cliché thing I had ever done—driving out to L.A. to chase my dreams. The suspense was building as the movie of my life dramatically unfolded. I wasn't sure if I was more energized or terrified by the realization that it was finally time to set back out to sea. It's a good thing I didn't know about the monsters along the way, or I would have crawled right back into bed.

28

ACROSS THE DESERT

As I drove, the forced silence soothed me into a hypnotic state of inner peace, which morphed into the unexpected viewing of my entire life. In fact, it flashed before me in such a slow, controlled fashion that it was like sitting alone in a theater watching a slideshow.

Regardless of the fact that I was holding the metaphoric controller to each passing scene, I observed in a detached and submissive manner. *I always played it off so tough, with so much pain trapped inside. Most people didn't know me. I never showed most of them, and I still haven't. It's still being revealed to me.*

My twenties were the main theme of this theatrical showing, as they had been jam-packed and wildly unpredictable. I had always known that I should get everything out of my system while I was young because my career was going to take over my life. My feisty spirit wouldn't have had it any other way.

I ached to be able to sit my twenty-year-old self down and tell her to listen to her gut—always. I wished for her to not be so hard on herself and to not care what people think. I wanted to hug her and whisper, "Slow down" and "You're enough," in her ear.

I imagined shaking her and telling her to listen to her inner warning system and to never ignore those red flags. Sadly, I wanted to tell her not to be so trusting of people and to break from the mold and question things sooner. She deserved to know how many times she would stubbornly ignore her gut—which would send her spiraling off track. Regret surfaced.

Reflecting on about a million situations that I wish I had behaved differently in, there was also an understanding now that these events served a purpose. That's part of life, and the mistakes had become points of reference, wisdom, and an impressive repertoire of insane stories. There were obviously many things that I wish I had handled with the polar opposite actions and etiquette, but the past doesn't move. *Geez, it's like I was born to make mistakes.*

Each passing hour slipped away like a microsecond, revealing flashes of uncovered truth. Completely detached from everyone, it was as if I lived on another planet. I knew what other people were thinking of me and could feel their confusion and level of discomfort. Sadly, I could feel the judgment. I always can. There was no blaming them, though. I was all over the place, thanks to my perplexing tour guide.

I wish that I could say the drive was completely uneventful. I wish that I could say that no one bothered me and that people just let me exist in my heightened state of peace, exploration, and anonymity. I wish I could say that—but here comes the creeper.

29

NIGHTMARE IN TEXAS

It was an uncomfortable ninety degrees out, and I was ready to call it a day. As I sat at the counter of a very crowded restaurant, a man sat down next to me, and my body froze in response to his energy. *Oh, boy, something is really off here.*

He was trying to get me to notice that he was looking at pictures of a family on his social media. He repeatedly glanced at me to see if I was noticing him. He wanted me to think of him as a family man, and therefore safe in his presence. My dead stare should have informed him that I wasn't interested in talking. It should have.

He predictably tried to engage me in conversation, and my responses were short and disinterested. I was trapped waiting for my food. I wasn't in the mood to converse with anyone, especially someone that I was already suspicious of. So I just secretively watched from under the brim of my hat as behavioral red flags fired off.

He continued to talk at me as he told me a detailed story about his family relocating. *Oh, yeah? Where are they?* My body sensed the lie.

He then showed me an app on his phone that listed off the hotels in the local area. His screen was only showing three of them, and he nonchalantly asked me which one I was staying in. *Ha. Yeah right, buddy. Nice try, creep.*

He continued to try to get information from me, and I coldly interjected. When that didn't work, he proceeded to ask me neutral questions that would have seemed harmless to most women. It was easy to see how he could earn someone's trust. He was trying too hard to appear nice and innocent. On full alert, I struggled to block his energy as it continued to reveal his intentions.

He had closed body language for most of the one-sided conversation, but then he stood up. He was intentionally, and obviously, leaning into my personal space now—nearing my intimate space. There were a hundred people in the room, and it was broad daylight, so I was safe but well aware of his behaviors.

My stomach was hardening, though, and rising to my throat. He was testing my boundaries, and I knew it. He wanted to see if I was comfortable with him or afraid of him. Only suspecting of him, it didn't matter whether I was being polite—I just stared straight ahead and didn't flinch.

It wasn't until he sat back down and whipped around to face me that we made direct eye contact for the first time. My blood went cold. His sickening being and the grotesqueness of his prior actions in life coursed through me. It was the strongest physical reaction to a person yet.

His entire demeanor changed as it became obvious that he had actively targeted me. He was now completely open and leaning toward me. I will never forget the way my stomach flipped. This instant nauseous feeling was new to me. I wasn't scared, just physically ill in response.

His eyes were light blue and glossed over in a way that I can only describe as a child molester's eyes. They were begging me to trust him, and my body reacted with instinctual revolt.

I had to test him to see how he responded to me leaving. I slowly stood up to see how he reacted to my actions, and sure enough, he jerked in animalistic response. *Yup, I had a feeling you would do that.* I forced a reassuring smile and calmly readjusted in my chair. He didn't want me to leave, which meant that I had to outsmart him.

There was no way I would let him follow me out, because I didn't want him to see my car. I was crawling out of my skin and wanted to expose him to everyone. He disgusted me. I had to get away. His energy was suffocating me.

Then the waitress mentioned that it was Father's Day, the perfect opportunity to vanish. I casually acted like I had forgotten to call my dad and asked her to save my seat so I could step outside and call him. I smiled and let them know I would be right back. Having already paid, I walked out and then bolted.

My body had alerted me of potential risk before, and the energetic threat of danger had stayed with me for hours. A couple of times there was a powerful sensation of being choked, regardless of no one touching me. Nothing was as severe as this, though.

The panic expanded as I started to process what my body was telling me. I was shaking and scared out of my mind, despite the fact that I was in no danger at all. There were people everywhere, but the feeling wouldn't budge. His horrific energy had latched on.

I ran up to my room and locked the door—checking it repeatedly. My body ached with electric shocks. I was cursing the fact that I could feel other people. It had frequently been painful, but rarely did it scare me. *Why do I have to feel so deeply?*

While calm in the restaurant, it had all caught up to me afterward. His creepy eyes were ingrained in my mind. I couldn't shake it off. Sleep was impossible. The threat of a nightmare with him in it was more troubling than the idea of sleep deprivation on such a massive road trip. Irrational thoughts had my guard up.

On top of everything, there was a thunderstorm that was making me question whether the flimsy glass windows would break. It was like accidentally stepping into a scene straight out of a horror film. Any attempt at comfort was in vain, as I obsessively counted down the minutes until dawn. Some restless sleep finally graced me.

A deep breath escaped me as the car door slammed behind me the next morning. Then my eyes darted to a note on my windshield. *What? How? Oh, no, he somehow found me. Is he watching me right now?*

I reluctantly opened the door and snagged it. There was instant relief to see that it wasn't from the creep the night before. Instead, it was from a random guy who had passed me on the highway and waved at me the day before. *What? Are you kidding me? Yeah, buddy, that sure was a special moment for me too— how did you find me? That was hours before I stopped.*

Apparently he had seen my car in the parking lot and felt compelled to give me his number and leave a note. Still not okay behavior but at least it wasn't the guy from the night before. I crumpled it up and took another deep breath. I wish I could say that's where the nightmare stopped. I really do. But cue the rabid wolf.

30

NIGHTMARE IN NEW MEXICO

Even miles of emptiness weren't comforting, as my eyes were fixated on the mirror to see if anyone was following me. It wasn't until hours later that the euphoric state began to return, thanks to some calming music and self-coaching. *I can't believe I took energy on that intensely. Why do I have to become the energy field next to me? Why?*

As I dropped off my luggage, a sense of déjà vu blasted me. It was the safest option in the middle of nowhere, but I still had a strange feeling. *Shake it off, it's time to relax and get some food.*

In search of a hearty meal, the surrounding security guards provided some comfort. The restaurants weren't open for another fifteen minutes, so I sat down nearby to wait it out. My plan was to eat and then hide in my room until the morning.

After a few moments, another couple sat close by, which helped me relax even more. A feeling of déjà vu washed over me again. We were all quietly watching the television, and I was just starting to fully overcome my shattered nerves when I saw him. *Oh, no, are you kidding me?*

It didn't take me more than a split second to know that this was a situation more alarming than the night before. There was immediate danger now. There was nothing but a brass railing separating me from the rest of the room. He was on the outside of the railing, circling me. Glaring at me. Targeting me.

He was wearing a worn white T-shirt, and his body language was very clearly a result of substance use and adrenaline. He was bouncing up and down in animalistic anticipation of the attack. He had a deadlock stare on me and wasn't veering his eyes in any other direction. His energy chilled me to the core.

A subtle glance around to see if anyone else saw what was going on revealed that they were all looking away. *Wait, where are the security guards? Are you kidding me? How is no one noticing this? Where did the security guards go? They were just here.*

However, I was as relaxed as if we were filming a scene in a movie. Everything inside me slowed down as if I had been in that exact scenario before. Again, the déjà vu feeling flashed through me. I shook my head in disbelief that this was happening.

He was stalking me in the same way a wolf would before it closes in on a rabbit. I knew it was important for me not to react or show fear, as movement attracts movement. Just like a rabbit, if it starts to bolt—so does the wolf. So I tucked him into my peripheral vision as he circled me. He was pounding his fist into the palm of his other hand now, his stare intensifying. *Are you kidding me?*

My hand covertly slipped into my purse and pulled out my weapon in preparation for an attack. Having protection was certainly helping me override the fear, but more than anything, it was just habituated from rehearsing it in my mind so many times, as I had been advised in school.

I knew he was going to pounce with his level of adrenaline—his energy was confirming that. He was just waiting for an opportunity, and I was ready. He was circling me like I was his prey, and he didn't care who was watching. Surprisingly, everyone seemed to be actively ignoring it. *How is no one reacting to this?*

He then started to walk behind me, and I whipped myself around to glare him down, letting him know that I wasn't afraid but instead was aware of his threat. To my shock, I saw his eyes—they were black—literally black. Pure evil. A chill shot up my spine.

I stared him down as he plowed past me and went over toward the restrooms, his eyes locked on me the entire time. He was now stalking me from a distance, pacing back and forth. He was waiting for me to move as he bobbed around like a kid on a sugar high. His energy was impossible to block. His creepy smirk unforgettable. *He's just waiting for me to get up and out of everyone's view.*

Then it happened—an unexpected rush of security guards flooded the area. They came out of nowhere like a small SWAT team. Half of them chasing after the "rabid wolf," as I had accurately titled him, and the other half rushing toward me to alert me that I was about to be attacked. Again, it was just like a scene from a movie. Apparently they had been watching it on the security camera.

When it was finally safe, the few witnesses whipped toward me. They all had the same look of horror on their face, and they asked me if I had seen his eyes. *Ahh, so they had noticed. Nice of you to try to protect me!*

Sleep that night was again impractical but still not as chilling as the night before, which surprised me. *Why did this happen?*

Did it happen so that I can help teach women to be prepared by carrying a weapon? I'm so happy I wasn't looking down at my phone. Why does this feel so staged?

As I drove away, I was well aware that my eyes were trying to escape my head as if they were running scared from what they had just witnessed. My head scrambled in search of courage, and relief didn't surface until the "Welcome to California" sign came into view. There was a strange feeling in the air about where the journey was going, as well as an awareness that I was being blown in the right direction.

31

WELCOME TO BOOT CAMP

After a few days, it became evident that the fear was blocking the usual guidance I receive. I was completely alone. *I don't feel aligned here. There's resistance, yet I'm supposed to be here. Why? Why L.A.?*

"Go see Stephanie."

Finally, some guidance! We had been e-mailing back and forth, but I had hoped to meet up with her once I was settled. Then I figured that we could bounce ideas, get to know each other more, and see if there was something that we could work on together. *Hmm, maybe it is the right time for some reason.*

Stephanie and I met for dinner. I told her the stories about the spirits that had always been part of my life and how I had just *known* things. I was comfortable telling her my stories with spirits and my instincts. She was very knowledgeable in that area as well and provided so much clarity about being clairvoyant.

It got rather late, and she told me that I could crash at her place and kindly offered to let me stay there while I figured out what to do next. She set me up with an air mattress on the floor of her workout room, and she handed me a book about psychics. *I know this is the right direction, as random as this is.*

◊

Absurdly confused, I raced up to Sonoma within a few days to clear my head and analyze the idea of staying in a city that was so unnerving. I begged the Universe for guidance. *I don't know how to relay to my friends what is happening. I don't even understand what is happening. Will I ever stop spinning in this tornado?*

There was an invisible barricade up between my old life and this strange new reality. I was spiraling in a different direction and didn't know how to explain it. I was in a self-imposed bubble and couldn't stop floating down this instinctual path. I had to keep going through the maze and heading toward people who speak "the language." They had answers, and I desperately craved answers. There was no escaping the matrix, not without doing the work.

I had ventured into unknown territory, and because of this, I could sadly feel myself growing away from many people in my life. It was one of the greatest heartbreaks of the whole journey. Without my consent, I could feel people being yanked away from me, and a massive energy block would erupt between us. I couldn't even text or call. It was an impenetrable wall.

Needing more guidance, I called Dawn, and she told me that I should go back to L.A. to the woman who was helping me, without me mentioning her at all. It was obvious that she was referring to Stephanie. *Okay, Universe, if that's what you want, then that's what I will do. What in the world has my life become? Are you sure I can't move back up to Northern California now? May I skip to the end?*

32

SERIOUS STUDENT

Stephanie quickly fell into the role of spiritual guide, teacher, and friend, which was exactly what I had hoped for. It was as though she was prepping me for something. She was introducing me to so much truth so fast. Concepts, theories, teachers, and books were being blasted at me simultaneously. I was plowing through books as though it was my job.

We went to another radio show at Neil's house. Watching him read the guest's nonverbal language and digging deep to pull the truth out was, again, impressive. As inspired as I was, I didn't know how I could help, so it just seemed like a dead end. *What can I contribute? Universe, why am I here? Neil and his editor and I have a crazy past-life connection, but what do I know about this world?*

I did my best to anchor myself in this new harbor. However, when I did try to search for nearby apartments and jobs, I was dramatically blocked every single time. *Umm, what's going on?*

This was something I had never experienced before. It was happening at coffee shops that had excellent Internet connection. I would be on a site that worked perfectly fine and then I would try to do an apartment search, and it mysteriously wouldn't load the page. Then when I tried to go to a different website, it would immediately connect again.

There seemed to only be dead ends. I had quite a few interviews, and the behaviors of each and every interviewer were unexplainably bizarre. I would come back completely confused, with wacky stories and no job.

One interviewer looked puzzled and asked me why I would even want to work there. Another one was using power and intimidation techniques like crushing my hand when he shook it and staring me down while leaning forward on his desk. I kept calling home and saying, "Something is very wrong," despite not knowing what it was.

Meanwhile, the social conditioning continued to unravel, as I belly flopped down the rabbit hole of truth. The second half of the book was completed quickly, and when that finish line came into view, it only amped me up even more. *Keep going, and get this book done! Dawn did predict that the Universe had more things for me once the book was done—what could that be? What are the psychic and spiritual things she was talking about?*

The Palisades Park in Santa Monica was the other place that had a magnetic pull for me. I would gaze out at the ocean, trying to piece together the jigsaw in my head. *How can I best express myself in a unique way? How can I blend my passions? How can I inspire people? Please help me see my vision more clearly. This is so frustrating!*

I would get lost for hours observing the entertaining spectrum of humanity as I prayed for answers. I frequently met people who were traveling and had run out of money or veterans who just couldn't fit back into society. Their stories often inspired me and touched my heart. It made sense how this could happen. My soul felt for their aching souls.

The purest moments were witnessed in that park, from babies trying to walk, to people painting, to elderly couples in love, to old men playing checkers. People had the right idea as they danced, played, read books, indulged in their passions, worked out, relaxed, or literally slowed down to smell the roses. This was where I was at peace, not realizing that it was about to be wildly disrupted by an invisible serpent.

33

THE SERPENT SPINS

During this time, I was introduced to meditation and self-hypnosis recordings that opened my mind in ways that I couldn't comprehend. One day in meditation, I even heard a very clear whisper, "*The Rule Breaker*," in response to my question about what title to use—putting an end to more than a year of agonizing about it.

My addictive personality became obsessed with studying and experimenting with things like hemisphere synchronization, binaural beats, past-life regression, astral projection, guided imagery, and lucid dreaming. I was time warping with my meditation and going on mental journeys that were indescribable. *Reality* was distorted as this limitless world of magical exploration consumed me.

I learned how to reach people in their dreams and how to send messages energetically. My mind continued to stretch exponentially. Something was changing in every cell of my being. What was really significant was how much my dream states had changed, as I became lucid in them. Precognitive dreams became a more regular occurrence.

In retrospect, I was going too fast spiritually—'tis my nature. Between what I was learning about my past lives, my soul's purpose, and my ability to connect with my spirit guides, my whole foundation was rewiring. It was so disorienting. I felt cheated that this had never been shown to me before.

Then one day while meditating at the beach, I settled into position and closed my eyes. After a few moments of stillness, a blast of intense energy zapped me like a bolt of lightning—without the pain, of course. *Whoa! What is this?*

The energy spun around inside me like a coiled snake, claiming its new territory. It was like coming out of anesthesia, leaving me in a dizzy, confused, and rather silly state. My weakened body made it hard to focus, so meditating was no longer an option.

When I explained what had just happened, Stephanie identified it as the Kundalini spins. *Huh? The what?*

I learned that this was a spiritual awakening that involves stirring up trapped energy. Apparently many cultures actively try to release it, but it can also occur unexpectedly. It is triggered when a person is following their soul's authentic path, and it is released when they are ready and open to it. *Well, I guess meditation is paying off. Is this the trapped energy people keep mentioning?*

My energy would blast off and then crash hard. I was experiencing tingling and vibrating sensations and was often lightheaded. It was extremely trancelike. To say that this was an overwhelming experience is an understatement. My emotions were so polarized. I was out at sea in the thick of a storm.

Electronics began acting wackier around me than they normally do. Everything was short-circuiting—even me. *What does this mean? What do I do with this?*

This continued to happen spontaneously for months, only each time it was less and less intense and would rise up slowly. I would experience the same swirling within me as it eventually ended up as an explosive pressure at the top of my head, as if something were escaping.

Yes, I'm aware that this sounds bizarre, even fruity. The former version of me would have questioned such a claim. Somehow, I was on a spiritual retreat—in L.A. of all places—unclear as to why this wasn't happening at a remote spiritual sanctuary.

34

A SURPRISE VISITOR

It was very obvious that I wasn't myself. Everything was so cloudy. I tried to create a sense of normalcy, but I ached for the real me. I missed my friends terribly. I wanted to leave. My gut, however, demanded I stay. It was as though there was a force keeping me there.

Shortly afterward, an opportunity to be a dating and relationship expert fell into my lap in a very synchronistic way. The creator of the show explained that they had unlimited funding by a very successful music producer and that they wanted to shoot the pilot in a couple months.

The other host was tentatively a well-known TV dating and relationship expert, who was apparently interested in the show. *Well, okay, this sounds very fitting for the TV crew prediction. Is this it?*

Things continued to open up spiritually. One night, I picked out a meditation recording and got into a relaxed state to slow my mind down. My eyes were closed for a few moments until a blast of blinding light forced them to rip open. *Umm, what in the world is this?*

I whipped my head to the left and couldn't believe what I was looking at. My eyes squinted in protective response. It was the most beautiful thing I had ever seen. My mouth dropped as the realization that I was looking at a ball of light began to sink in. It was more stunning and intricate than a chandelier. It was a few feet in diameter and as bright as a star. A flood of peace and warmth filled the room. Overwhelming love consumed every crevice within me. *Is that an angel?*

Some might have described it as an angel, and that's the sense that I got. It was a ball of glowing energy. It lit up the whole room, and after just a few moments, it was gone. *Wow, that was incredible. Whoa!*

It was the most shockingly gorgeous thing I had ever seen. It was mind blowing, and I wished for all people to see something so pure. *Seriously, thank you, Universe! Wow, how amazing!* Little did I know that was the high before a gut-wrenching low— an unprecedented low—a writer's nightmare.

35

A WRITER'S NIGHTMARE

I had heard about a writer's high and imagined it to feel similar to a runner's high; either way, this was clearly it. The finish line was in eyeshot.

The manuscript had just been sent to Stephanie for a second opinion. It was structured as a book of hard-learned lessons, which included stories from my journey throughout to emphasize my messages. *Am I actually almost done?*

Then it happened. Stephanie commented on the fact that the stories were the strongest part of the book. She advised me to tell my whole story so that readers could learn the lessons through them. The punch-in-the-gut reaction to her words confirmed it was the truth. *That would mean starting over. Wait, what? Uh-oh! No, no, no!*

She also said that it needed more vulnerability—and again, I knew she was right. I knew it instantly. I knew I had to start over, and I knew I wasn't all right. That was obvious.

Already running on empty, this meant the roller-coaster ride was now stuck upside down. Naturally, I panicked. It was like telling a marathon runner just before the finish line that they have to start over—the mind can't process that. It doesn't want to conceive a cruel joke like that. *Start at word one? I can't breathe.*

Quitting right then and there was the most appealing option, as a flood of anger and resentment poured in to protest the idea of starting from scratch. *I can't do this. This is impossible. No book? Start over? I can't do this!*

How anticlimactic. How traumatizing. Calculating the hours of time and energy invested into that book only amplified my broken heart. I had dreamed about its future and wanted to watch it grow. I had put my whole life on hold for it. Everything in me shut down; the system had collapsed. *No book? Nothing to show for all my hard work? Start over? I'm going to lose it.*

On top of that, it became obvious that the TV show wasn't going anywhere. That, of course, wasn't helping. I had been so close to my dreams, and now I had nothing. I had to get out of there. So I booked a flight to New York. My whole world was spinning. The grieving had begun. *How can I start over?*

There wasn't a person in my life who understood me at that point. There were people I love who tried, but no one would ever understand the depths of how far I fell.

I would sit in my car for hours with a blank stare, trying to figure out how to possibly keep piecing together this frustrating puzzle. *I'm broken. I'm lost. I want to quit. This is too hard. I just don't have the energy to care anymore! What is the point of all this? Why do I feel like this? Why is this so painful? Damn it! I can't do this! How can I relay such meaningful experiences and lessons? How can I do justice to this story? Am I even a storyteller?*

I couldn't talk to anyone because people wanted to know what was going on with me, and I had no idea. They wanted to know when the book would be done, and that was just salt in the wound.

The heaviness on me made depression seem like a breeze. It felt like I had an extra hundred pounds weighing me down.

When I wanted to say or do certain things, I would either be verbally paralyzed or would say or do the polar opposite—as if I had no control over my words or behaviors anymore. I was completely brain-dead and had serious memory loss. The most basic things were beyond perplexing to me.

Stephanie had asked me if dark spirits were messing with me several times, but that wasn't something that I was willing to consider. I was also too disoriented to grasp that concept. Of course it terrified me, and the denial revved up.

Unfortunately, I got my answer though. One night, I was startled awake out of a deep sleep. With a chilling energy in the air, a dark, wispy *thing* blasted out of my mouth and shot across the room. The air went ice cold and I was left trembling in shock, unable to move. It was a real-life nightmare, and I wish it weren't true.

I also wish that's where it stopped, but it was now official that dark spirits were messing with me, trying to stop me from fulfilling my mission, and ruining my life. I should have known. Things had been strange all throughout my life and increasingly bizarre since Thailand. The destruction of my life continued with me as the passenger.

36

REBOOT AND REBUILD

I was in a well. I had never been there before. Pitch black. Dead silent. The lights were out. It was the kind of alone that maddens you because you just don't know how to get yourself out of it, and you wonder if you ever will. *I can't do this. I was just about to regain my life and fulfill my purpose. I'm dead. I'm not able to function.*

Depression had engulfed me at various times before, but this was a new dimension of mental and emotional alienation. This was inner-imprisonment, and there was no one who could help me escape. *I can't see the light at the end of the tunnel. I'm lifeless. I can't do this. I want to disappear. Did I disappear?*

I was a wreck when I got home, and there was no way to hide it from my family. They noticed the effects of my unintentional malnourishment and exhaustion. I was struggling to just take care of myself. My fingernails were brittle, my muscle mass was fading, and my hair was dull and dry.

There was no way to express myself. I was screaming from the depths of my soul, but the sound waves couldn't exit my mouth. I was being held captive, in plain sight.

I missed my life. I was a million miles away from everyone, and I didn't have a signal to reach them. Even standing next to my family, I might as well have been on a spaceship. *I miss you all! I'm not myself, so I can't be with you. I'm nothing more than a ghost right now—absolutely empty. I lost my damn mind.*

I was grieving the *loss* of my book. A part of me was missing. It was exhausting to realize that I was now in the fight of my life, the fight for freedom and my dreams. It wasn't about money; it was about achieving what I had set out to do. It was about fulfilling my purpose and inspiring others. It was about coming back to life. *Ahh, my body is so heavy. Come on, baby, you gotta get up! You can do this; you always do. You have to get these messages out to the world. You have to raise awareness and help people.*

I didn't have a clue what to say to my family and friends. "Hey guys, I'm back at square one"; "Hey guys, everything I worked so hard for is gone"; "Hey guys, I want to quit"; "Hey guys, something is attacking my energy field, and I'm losing touch with reality." There were no words, just defeat. *No, no, no—this can't be happening.*

Then at my lowest moment, as if he could somehow sense it, my sweet sociopath sent a text that read, "I would love to catch up." This time he had poked me too many times. I suddenly wanted to confront him in person and even tried to.

An animalistic fire lit up in me, and I wanted to channel my pain toward him. I was craving closure, but I was also well aware that he was too cowardly to see me face to face. He was playing his usual games. Anger was pounding on the door, and I was doing my best to keep it from busting in. The rage was inevitable—and primal. Little did he know that by poking at me, he was fueling me when I needed it the most.

Giving up was no longer an option. So I wiped the slate clean. It was time to rebuild and begin the restructuring of the new book. I'll never fathom where the strength to start over came from. Fighting the urge to give up, I kept finding a new watering hole of faith and courage just as I was about to keel over. *I'm coming out of this with the book no matter what it takes. Pick yourself up. This is bigger than you!*

37

READY, SET, WRITE

The channeling floodgates finally opened. I was plowing through the book now, and there was no denying the drastic improvement. I was actually grateful for starting it over. Just as importantly, writing it this time was fun. For the first time in my life, I felt like a true writer. I had found my niche. *I'm a storyteller! Didn't see that coming! Although I'm not sure how, I love telling stories! Wow, this is the book that I had always known I would write—the actual book!*

Recently it seemed like there were twelve-ton anchors on each limb as I struggled to climb the mountain to my dreams. That heaviness had finally let up enough to allow me to gain some momentum.

The book was now caught up to the present times. I was nothing more than a character in a book. It was my identity. It was my obsession. It was annoying everyone around me, especially me. I had been reading it over and over for months, a cruel, and necessary, process. The relentless nightmares were on full blast.

However, laced throughout, there were repeating dreams about a stunning beach area that felt familiar, yet I didn't recognize it. It was so real that I ached to be there as it flashed in and out. It was a light at the end of the tunnel. A new life was deeply sensed, although I was clueless as to where it would begin. Either way, the roller coaster was unstuck and in motion again, slow motion.

38

WELCOME TO PARADISE

As I looked around the Boston airport, a deep breath helped me settle into the realization that I had absolutely no idea what my plan was—other than heading back to California. All I knew is that it was time to leave L.A. and head north. That alone was worth a smirk.

As I drove away from spiritual boot camp, the awareness of how much my sanity had derailed consumed me. I was now leaving with knotted thinking that had to be sorted. A new version of myself was emerging through the fog, but there was a long road of healing ahead. I wasn't even close to feeling like myself. *Okay, back out to sea. Where will I wash up? Is it time for Northern California again? I hope so!*

Hours slipped away as I floated up the coast. I had told Stephanie I kept sensing beach towns and art galleries. I didn't know why, but it kept surfacing.

Then, for no reason, my phone died, despite it being completely charged. So this meant that I had no GPS. My only clue was to head north. *How typical, my electronics never work. Okay then, you lead the way, Universe.*

Shortly after, I snapped out of my autopilot state as I realized that I was exiting the highway. There had been a sudden jerk of the wheel, as though someone else had made that decision for me. *Whoa, why am I stopping here? What is this place?*

A flush of reassuring heat surged through me as I drove by a hotel and a nearby restaurant. My inner guidance then whispered the next steps. *Hmm, interesting.*

So I checked in, walked into my room, and yanked the curtains open. As corny as this sounds, dolphins started dramatically jumping out of the sparkling water as if they were greeting me. Rabbits scurried by, and a humming bird started zipping around me as a flock of pelicans flew by in slow motion. *What in the world! Am I in a cartoon?*

I walked around the property and was seduced by the bright flowers, as I discovered caves, exotic beaches, animals, and countless romantic settings. It was instant peace. *This is obviously the place I was tapping into!*

The next morning, I flew out of bed to go meditate on the beach, and absolutely no one was around. I might as well have been on a deserted island, hidden from the world. Between the soaring birds and the seals sunbathing on the rocks, it was hypnotic. I put my headphones in, and unprecedented dancing flooded out. *Wow, I'm really channeling my pain. Dancing has something to do with all this, but what?*

With every mile of exploration, I fell more and more in love. Everyone was engaging in outdoor activities, people were authentically laughing, drivers were waving and smiling, and the fire inside me was spreading rapidly. Synchronicities were darting at me in every direction. *Well, I guess this beat-up gem washed up in paradise! Yeah, baby!*

The navigation system still wasn't working, so I was driving along solely based on my instincts. The car seemed to drive on its own and ended up at a nearby golf course. *Hmm, that's weird. I'm going there soon, but I don't golf. Whatever, I'm just coasting along on this adventure.*

I then drove a few exits down and parked. As I walked down to the beach, I stopped dead in my tracks. *Whoa! No way!* Straight ahead of me was the real-life version of the dream I had back when I was in New York. It wasn't similar—it was exact.

I recognized it immediately. It was the view of the ocean, the stores, and the pier that I had longed for from the recurring dream. *Precognitive dreams are really trippy. This must be why I have déjà vu all the time. I can't believe the messages I've been getting. I'm obviously where I'm supposed to be.*

As I was walking around, in a matter of ten minutes I heard three different people talking about a local restaurant, and I knew that was the spot for dinner.

I instantly made some friends, and by the end of the night, they offered me a ticket to a blue's festival the following day—which was going to be at the same golf course I had been pulled to. *Ha, of course!*

Before the concert, we met up for lunch, and the couple next to me instantly struck up conversation. Within just a short time, they kept saying, "We met you for a reason." When I mentioned a nearby town, she blurted out, "You have to stop at the art galleries." She enthusiastically repeated it a few times.

Then, to my surprise, she reached into her purse and pulled

out two coupons for a winery. There was no hiding the shock on my face.

The image was exactly the same couple that I had on my vision board. I had just typed in "couple drinking wine," and that image had resonated with me. The twilight music was playing in my head as my attraction experiment was lighting up.

To top it off, the blues festival was mind blowing. We were all lost in the sensational performances. People were actually using jazz hands. Couples were lost in each other as they danced. *Is this the island of happy dancing people? What is this place?*

There wasn't a cell phone to be seen. I was looking at true happiness. People were skipping, playing with beach balls, hula-hooping, dancing, and even doing cartwheels and headstands. It was a world of "grown-ups" who were playing like children. It was raw truth. *Ahh, back to basic human nature!*

From live painting to enjoying delicious food to simply blowing bubbles—everyone was just playing. The gender lines were blurred. Women weren't being objectified. Natural talent was in every corner, and I was thrilled.

Instead of goofy designer brands, I was seeing motivating phrases, such as "It's time for peace" and "Happiness is a choice." *Imagine if we modeled this Pacific playground more than the illusion of L.A.. Imagine if we stopped allowing the media to condition us to feel insecure. There's too much unrealistic pressure on women, and it's ruining lives. Imagine if we realized how unsocial all this social media is. Imagine if we took the reins. Imagine if we united and moved in a new direction.*

Laughter filled the air. The synergy, the abundance, and the magic left me weightless and fueled with gratitude. *Life should be more like this! We all need to get back in touch with our inner child. We need to connect more with the source. We need to play!*

39

ART CHANGES LIVES

Taking the advice of the couple at lunch, the nearby town they recommended was next on the intuitive itinerary. Within moments of being there, a male energy suddenly blasted me. *Who in the world is this now?*

So I started strolling around again, and that inner *ding* signaled when I walked by a restaurant. *Hmm, guess I'm going there soon.* I hadn't walked into any of the art galleries, but as I was about to pass another one, my spirit guides yanked me in.

I laughed at the realization that the guy who greeted me was the energy field that I had just tapped into. We started chatting, and he made a nearby recommendation for food—at none other than the restaurant I had just been drawn to. He advised me to sit outside by the creek and to get the salmon bisque. *Well, okay then. I'm starving! That's a fun clue.*

After a few moments, I thanked him and left without

exchanging information. I had no doubt that I would see him again. He was an old mate for sure.

So I went to the restaurant that he suggested and got a seat out on the balcony, overlooking the water, and ordered the salmon bisque.

Then, sure enough, the guy from the art gallery walked in and sat at a nearby table. I ended up waving him over, and we both smirked—just like a scene from a movie—probably a cheesy one, though.

That evening, I sat by a fire pit trying to grasp how uplifting the last few days had been. I had simply surrendered, yet I had made friends, gone to a concert, had a social life, found the place where I wanted to settle down, been on a "date," made a special connection, interviewed for and been offered a job—all by being happy and going with the flow, nothing more. *Look at that: technology played no part in this at all.*

The next time I saw Kevin, I explained to him that I wasn't getting involved with anyone because my focus was my book, and I wasn't myself. We both agreed that we still wanted to spend time together, and we knew that if our friendship was supposed to go somewhere, it naturally would down the road. So he offered an extra room, and my attempt to regain my sanity began.

40

THIS IS RANDOM

Within two weeks of discovering this new land, one of the business guys from the product I had been involved with randomly reached out to me. It had been more than a year since I had heard from Mike, and he told me that he wanted to talk to me about a business opportunity.

However, I just brushed it off to the side. He informed me that he was passing through the area in about a week, but I wasn't planning on seeing him—he wasn't exactly my favorite person. *No thanks, Universe. I'd rather not open that door again.*

A couple of days later, in the middle of editing, I had an overpowering pull toward an area more than half an hour away. I reluctantly followed the magnetic yank to the small town and ended up in front of an energy store. So I strolled on in.

Then a woman came out of her office and told me that if I needed anything to just knock on the door because she was on the phone. With no intention of getting a reading, confusion was inevitable. *Seriously, why am I here?*

After a few minutes, she came back out and said, "I'm sorry to bother you, but I am getting strong messages to give you," without saying that to anyone else in there.

Before responding, she said, "You just met a guy, and there is a big connection. You also just moved in with him, but you'll be leaving soon." She officially had my attention.

She also mentioned that there was so much business, money, and people in my vortex but that they couldn't come in because I was pushing them all away. She proceeded to tell me that I had become very confused about everything when I was living in L.A. and that I had energy that was trapped within me. *Yeah, I know I do. I've heard this before. I don't know how to unblock it! I'm suffering because of that.*

I knew the fear of failure had tripped me up. That fear had transitioned into fear of success paired with fear of dark energetic attacks. Either way, the fear was ruining my life, and I needed help. *I know I've been subconsciously self-sabotaging too. I'm chasing my dreams and pushing them away. I'm tired of dream chasing. I'm just tired. Tired and scared of where this is going—or not going. Tired of the force trying to stop me.*

One of the predictions was about living in a house where my business was downstairs, and there was a camera crew. *Well, this sounds familiar. When is this going to happen? I know the TV show concept that I want, but I don't know how to make it happen. Can I please just live in these predictions?*

She then mentioned that I would be signing a contract, that I would be getting published, that I would end up in a position of management and leadership, and that the book would be as big as I think it will be. *Okay, I've heard this, but how?* She was then adamant about me meeting up with Mike, as she described him flawlessly.

She kept telling me that I was psychic, that my gut was never wrong, and that I needed to stop doubting myself. She also mentioned that I needed to pay attention to the messages in my dreams.

It was baffling how much of what she was saying lined up with Dawn's predictions; at some points, it was word for word. She even brought up the fact that I had not been ready for the radio show in L.A. and that the timing hadn't been right. She told me to reach out to them and Neil Strauss when I was ready.

Afterward, Mike and I met at a coffee shop, and we talked about the book. His response was simply, "Wow, I wasn't expecting this. So you want to get published?" and I said, "Yes." So he said, "Consider it done." He then told me that he would contact some people and find the right person to help me. *Wow, this is so random. Are you sure this is the direction I should be going in? Something feels off.*

41

AND WE'RE MOVING

Immediately afterward, Mike invited me to Beverly Hills to meet the publishing coach he had found, Matt.

When we met up, Mike brought up a TV show that he was working on, which involved chefs from around the world, and he had decided that he wanted me to be the host. He listed off high-profile people who were involved, had a set location, and was specific about my role in it all. *Well, that's interesting, considering the premise of my TV show idea. Is this the camera crew that was predicted?*

As the struggling artist, I told Mike that I had already invested everything in the journey and the book that I could. He agreed to invest in me so that Matt could be my publishing coach. They signed a contract, and we got straight to work.

Without me mentioning a word about a specific publishing house, Matt told me that he was targeting one in particular—the only one that was on my vision board. He also said that when he called them, they said that my book sounded like the kind of book they would publish. *Wow, is it finally all happening?*

42

A SHARP JERK

The pressure to get my messages out there was only amplifying. My inner battle, however, was about how to publish the book. There were the variables of giving away most of my profits and being told how to do my book, and I was concerned that a publishing house would be working against my instincts. However, I just moved in the direction things seemed to be going in.

I was advised to get professional headshots and was informed that we would be shooting the pilot for the show in a few weeks. I scrambled to keep up.

So there I was with everything finally sent off to the publishing houses, my professional photos and a confident mind-set heading into my first TV exposure. Everything was perfectly on track, and I finally felt confident and ready.

Everything was in motion—I was riding high on momentum. At least until it came crashing down in a quick instant. At the last minute, I was told that the whole TV project wasn't going to work out at this time. *Are you kidding me? Everything sounded so finalized. What is with this cat-and-mouse game? I don't want to play anymore.*

I was devastated because my sister just happened to be visiting the week that we were going to film. I was going to surprise her by driving up the coast, pulling up to the mansion, and walking in to start filming. Instead, my heart cracked a little deeper. *Again, is anything real in this industry? Ahh, this is so painful! Why are things so close to what I'm visualizing but not happening?*

To push me over the edge, when my sister did visit, we were very obviously attacked by dark spirits. This time it was even more drastic and traumatizing. In the blink of an eye, we went from euphoric and energetic to zapped and soulless.

Without exaggerating, we went from a lovely ocean-side lunch to hopping in our car with huge smiles so that we could find a majestic beach that only locals knew about. We were revved up to go hiking and exploring. It was absolute perfection.

Then at the exact same time, we switched from filled with happiness to zombie mode. We were unable to function, and we had to skip our adventure.

We couldn't form thoughts and could hardly speak. Barely conscious, we were pinned down in bed, just listening to everyone laughing and playing on the beach to the live music. Ice cream was even flavorless, which had never happened before, even in our worst moments. We didn't know that was possible. It's ice cream!

We called it "going dumb" and "hell on earth." At one point, she blurted out that she was going to jump off a cliff, and because my thinking wasn't mine, I didn't even react.

My sister, a marathon runner, could barely walk ten feet. We didn't have control over our bodies, our speech, or our free will.

Our souls kept coming and leaving for about twenty-four hours at the exact same time.

When we were in public, people walked by us as if we were invisible. We sat in the middle of a busy restaurant for forty-five minutes, and no one saw us. Our souls were tortured, as we had been dragged to hell's headquarters. It was maddening. We parted ways sobbing and basically lifeless.

It took many days for it to start wearing off, as we slowly returned to our natural state. Her fiancé commented that it wasn't her that returned from California. It was radically traumatizing, and it took weeks to even vaguely recover emotionally. It was guaranteed to haunt me eternally.

It was obvious that other people around me were being attacked too, and it was always at my happiest moments. *They* would use people I love against me while we both said things we would never normally say and then silence us when we had important things to say. It was light years beyond exhausting, and it was impossible to trust people anymore.

My technology was being wiped out aggressively, I could barely eat, and my behaviors were so bizarre. Nothing made sense as I continued to be the strapped-in passenger of my distorted life, too numb to have coherent thoughts and too weary to understand one drop of what was happening. Inside, I was begging to die. Often pleading.

There was no denying that I was impaired socially and occupationally. I was so beat down. I would act childlike and helpless when I needed to be professional and speaking my truths. I couldn't communicate or focus. I often ended up in the fetal position, spinning.

Reality continued to become more of a blurred concept. Now knowing more about my purpose, I didn't want to fulfill it in some ways—in many ways. In fact, I was loathing it. I wanted to escape.

I felt the world on my shoulders and the collapse of my inner strength under the pressure. The writer's block was like having my head in a vise. The roller coaster was jerking me around aggressively, and I needed help. No one knew how to help me, though.

Feeling hopeless, I decided to see an acupuncturist that many people had been raving about in that area. Ms. Erika's intuitive and healing nature was immediately undeniable, and she lifted my vibrations significantly. I was safe opening up to her, and she began playing the role of therapist, doctor, mentor, and friend in my life. She was a beam of light and an instant blessing.

Meanwhile, the Universe was plotting to send me the most random lineup of characters to guide me, change me, and add to the bizarreness that is my life. I certainly wouldn't have believed it if I had advance notice, not for a second. *Let the scavenger hunt continue.*

43

OBVIOUS SIGNS

It was additionally draining waiting to hear from the publishing houses. During this time though, author Dr. Wayne Dyer kept showing up in my life in extremely synchronistic ways. I threw that sign in the ever-growing pile of things that were confusing me at this time.

Then an e-mail from OWN, Oprah Winfrey's Network, showed up in my inbox. This wasn't the first time, but it was the first time I had opened one. It was to promote a Wayne Dyer speaking event in L.A. in a few weeks.

"Buy a ticket."

Nah, I don't think so. I really didn't want to subject myself to driving to L.A.. However, there was such a strong sense that I was meant to attend—and that I was supposed to do it alone.

"Buy a ticket."

After debating this for about a week, that feeling became so strong that there wasn't a choice anymore. The urge was there for a reason. So the ticket was bought.

The intensity of the physical reaction to this decision became so consuming that I e-mailed myself that I was about to have an instant connection with someone there. This magnetic pull was overpowering. *Why is this energy stuff so intense and invasive? Why do I feel like I'm just getting started with it?*

What concerned me the most was that my voice was almost gone from rapping too much to Eminem as I worked on my own lyrics for spoken word, the predicted poetry. Combined with my hip-hop dancing, it was a therapeutic way to express myself. *Ahh, how can I connect with someone if I can't speak? Why do I always have to overdo it?*

$$\Diamond$$

When Friday finally rolled around, my head throbbed with anticipation. My palms were sweaty, my head was cloudy, and nausea swept over me. *This is so weird. Why the intense emotions?*

There were thousands of people there, and I just quietly walked around for a few moments before taking my seat—without talking to a single person. My nerves had a death grip. *Seriously, relax. Who in the world am I tapping into? Is it Wayne? They have explosive energy, that's for sure.*

As soon as Wayne started speaking though, my body recentered, and my focus dashed toward his words of wisdom. Every cell in my being confirmed that truth was echoing throughout the room.

He spoke of things like breaking away from social conditioning, the value of radical humility, being aligned in perfect love, and being highly spiritually evolved. As the queen of humility—and very clearly on a mission to break people away from social conditioning—my head just nodded with deep-rooted resonation. *I'm so grateful for this moment!*

I thought it was beautiful when he said, "We are all cells in the body of infinite intelligence." *When will we realize that we are all literally one? There is no degree of separation.*

At one point, Wayne talked about a "Writing from your soul" conference in Maui, and inner zaps of electricity got my attention. I jotted it down and put a star next to it. *Hmm, why do I feel like I'm going to that?*

Epiphanies bounced around the room, as his wisdom flicked the lights on for those in search of answers. He was doing what I want to do: storytelling, inspiring, teaching, waking people up, and using humor and wit to do it all. At one point he sarcastically said, "Please. Please try to understand how little I care." I knew I would be quoting that one. *How am I ever going to get my scared self on that stage? I want to do what he does! How, though?*

Wayne was absolutely hilarious, and his ability to engage the audience was undeniable. I truly appreciated how he used his personal stories to execute his messages. His inner battles with his vices resonated deeply—his vulnerability was something I admired greatly.

One thing that I noticed was that the average age of the crowd was at least a decade or two older than me. *Where are the twenty-year-olds? Hmm, I'm here to bridge this gap. How do I do this, Universe?*

As he finished speaking, I became lightheaded as anxiety coursed through my body again. *Why am I sweating? Go away, anxiety!* I knew I was supposed to make something happen, but I had no idea what that meant. *Why am I here, Universe? What do you want from me? Who is it that I'm here to meet?*

My inner magnet was being dragged across the room. The only thing I could think of was to run backstage, even though

I didn't have a voice to explain my odd behaviors. There was just an overpowering pull toward Wayne. That, and Eminem's "Lose Yourself" was playing in my head—the main song that had captured my voice.

"Stand by the stage."

Umm, why? Oh, no, am I about to run backstage and make myself seen? Ahh, I can't do this. Why is my stomach doing flips? Why am I so nervous? I kept looking around to see if people were going to intervene, but they were just clearing out. I was freaking out for no apparent reason.

I could see Wayne behind the curtain. Security was trying to clear out the last few people who remained. Then I glared backstage again. *Oh, wow, this is my moment. Something has to happen right now. I can feel it! I know I'm supposed to meet someone, and almost everyone is gone. Damn it, gut, what are we doing? You drive me crazy sometimes!*

44

INTERCEPTION

I had my eyes on those stairs as if they might flee at any moment. *What in the world am I doing? This is ridiculous!* My stomach was bracing itself for how badly this could backfire. There was no walking away now; I'd always wonder "What if?" Then my foot lifted, and my body started to propel forward. The nerves vanished. *Oh, well, I have nothing to lose.*

That's when I heard a very simple "Hi." That was it. She just said hi; her energy handled the rest. We looked at each other, smiled, and without a word, embraced in a hug. Ashley was the energy field I had tapped into. We both let out some tears of recognition. *This is really wild. Ugh, what now? I can barely talk, yet I have so much to say! Who is she?*

Then another woman approached us, and we started walking out toward the lobby. Once we got there, Hawaiian leis were put on Ashley and me, and we took pictures in front of the Hay House Publishing backdrop.

They invited me to dinner, and it was at that time that I discovered that they both knew Wayne personally. *Wow, I can't believe that I magnetized people that close to him. I'm really getting the hang of this gift, as confusing as it is. I just need to figure out how to utilize it.*

As if this wasn't mind blowing enough for me, her phone rang at that moment, and I saw her caller ID. *What? Wayne Dyer is calling her?*

They spoke for a few minutes and almost made plans to meet up but decided to wait until tomorrow. She said, "I love you," and hung up.

When she got off the phone she sent him the picture of us with the Hawaiian leis on. Ashley then said, "Well, tonight I am staying at an overnight Korean spa, would you like to come?" *Here in L.A.? I've never heard of that here. How can I say no?* My whole body was on fire. *Wow, life is so random! Okay, let the Asian-themed adventure continue.*

45

ESCAPE TO ASIA

The spa was the most authentic Asian experience that I had encountered since my trip there. The still silence granted us permission to hear ourselves think. *Ahh, an escape from this loud world. The silence is so comforting.*

We enjoyed meditation, Kundalini yoga, and the saunas. Most people were asleep at this point, so we basically had the themed rooms to ourselves. Ashley told me that she kept hearing the word *believe* in reference to the people in my life. She commented on people casting doubts on my dreams and declared that they needed to believe in me more. Sadly, she was spot on.

One of the most surreal moments was when we went to the rooftop, which was lit up with white lights. The vibe was calming, despite our location in the city of egoist madness. We shared similar stories of rising in consciousness, losing our friends because they cast doubts or other negative energies, shock that we had arrived at this spiritual level, and limitless gratitude for who we were becoming.

We had tears in our eyes as we felt understood and equally in shock that our lives had transcended from their original starting point. We had both endured a journey that was absolutely isolating to then collide with others who shared comparable paths of obstacles, challenges, and self-actualization. We were on the same frequency.

We determined that we were on a similar mission to light this world up and had been brought together for a reason. We each had our own blueprint to make that happen, but the purpose behind them was united.

Our youthful energy kept us up all night and then we crashed on our floor mats. After a couple of hours of rest, we said good-bye so that I could tackle the drive up the coast. It was time to leave the house of healing, but I knew I would see her again.

A couple of weeks later, Ashley randomly asked me to do her a favor and contact a former NFL player that I had never heard of. She wanted me to send him her business plan, and without reading it, I agreed to help her.

When I figured out how to contact him his mailbox was full so I couldn't leave a message. *Umm, who is this guy again? What do I say to him if he does answer?* This went on for a few days, and I was just about to give up on being able to speak to him directly.

Then on a Sunday morning, there was an urge to try one more time, and sure enough, he answered. This caught me off guard because the only expectation was to hear the same voicemail recording.

Immediately he blasted me with thought-provoking questions. It almost seemed like an interview. We ended up having a great conversation about higher consciousness, and some of his questions made my mind spin for answers.

A half hour later, I told him that I really enjoyed the conversation and that I wanted to talk in person at some point if that were possible. *That guy seemed cool. I'm feeling that magnetic pull toward him.*

Afterward, I sent him Ashley's business plan, but I didn't hear anything back. I didn't think too much of it, though. It was random, and I had zero expectations. So I just let it go.

At this time, the founder of a global leadership organization reached out randomly. I called her back and left a couple of messages but didn't hear anything in return. So I just let that go as well, even though there was an intense energy behind it. *That mission statement is in perfect alignment with what I want to do. Where is this going? Ahh, the suspense is killing me!*

46

INSPIRATION FROM LONDON

Editing was all I could think about, so outside of work, that was my focus. On one particular night, I was lost in the zone with some background music playing. When I'm in the flow, nothing yanks me out of it, especially music. This time, however, I kept hearing phrases that were in complete alignment with my book. The messages were demanding my attention. My whole body kept igniting with passion.

Each time I had to stop to see who was singing it. So I would pause the writing and get up to see who the artist was. Every time it was a hip-hop singer named Antix. He had been recommended to me several times and was one of my Pandora stations, but I had only heard a couple of his songs. I hadn't listened too closely to any of them yet.

The energetic pull toward him was undeniable, though. His lyrics paralleled many of my core beliefs. He was teaching the importance of questioning everything and exposing the truth. *Yes, yes, exactly!*

"Reach out to him."

There wasn't a moment of hesitation. I looked Antix up and sent him a message that read, "You are absolutely inspiring…I think we are on the same mission. The book I just wrote is about questioning everything. Please keep doing what you are doing…I want to help propel your messages!" There were no expectations, but he was added to my vision board. *That's a really strong magnetic pull too. Interesting…*

Then to my surprise, I heard back from him just a few hours later. He said, "You wrote a book about that? That is absolutely awesome." Then he asked me where I was in the United States.

When I told him California, he informed me that he would be coming to L.A. in just a few weeks. It just happened to be at the exact time that Ashley had invited me down there. *Are you kidding me? Ha, of course you are!*

Afterward, I dove a little deeper into his music at globalantix. com and couldn't grasp how much it was resonating with me. I loved that he let people listen to his music for free. He talked about personal struggles, barriers, and his journey. Lyrics about seeing through the illusion, saving the world, everyone being equal, chasing dreams, inner strength, shifting energy, freedom, being called crazy, losing friends who cast doubts, and how life is a game echoed throughout my home.

I could feel the fire and passion within him. It matched the heat that was trapped in me. It was the most I had related to an artist. I was staying up all night dancing and rapping. My trapped inner artist started exploding out of me. *Wow, I really want feedback at this point. I need to know if I have something here or if it's in my head. Who can I show this to? Seriously, L.A. again? Why are things yanking me back there?*

47

TO THE RECORDING STUDIO

The evening before meeting with Antix, or Alex, I was in a deep sleep. Then at about four in the morning, I shot out of bed and scrambled for my computer to record a dream that had just startled me awake. It was the only dream I had ever e-mailed myself about so that it was documented.

It involved Alex and some of his friends. We went from room to room, surrounded by Asian people. I ended up completely naked, vulnerable, and humiliated. That was just a minor clip, but it would be relevant momentarily—oddly relevant.

It's not possible to do justice to the intensity of the next part of the dream. The emotion behind it alone was extremely overwhelming. While experiencing it, I thanked the higher powers for showing me what they did—and ached to stay in that moment. Many attempts were made to return to that place the remainder of the night, but they were in vain. I barely slept.

◊

The next day, I met up with Alex at a restaurant by the Palisades Park. The city driving had stirred some anxiety, but that vanished when our energy fields synced up. We skipped right over the small talk and dove into a philosophical conversation, lobster rolls, white wine, and a stunning ocean view.

A few hours of global discussion confirmed that we had a similar mission to wake people up and get them to question everything in our "reality." We spoke a language—the one I want the world to be fluent in.

I couldn't help but notice the intensity and depth of his eyes— his soul had endured deep experiences. He was raw and real, his energy was confirming it. Respect was inevitable as he discussed seeing through the illusions and the media's intentions to manipulate women. Combined with his innate wit, humor, and intelligence, I was convinced I was sitting with a major force of influence in this world.

He had no idea how much he was inspiring me—he was literally making me feel less alienated. For some reason, I was instinctually protective of him. There was a sense of family. I just wanted to make him proud and advocate for him as much as possible. He was igniting a primal instinct, and my soul ached to show him my vision and inner artist. These were still painfully trapped, though.

I told Alex that he was the only artist that I have ever reached out to and commented on how perfect the timing had been with him coming out to L.A.. He then told me that he rarely visits that area and that I was the first "fan" that he ever agreed to meet up with. *Ha, meant to be.*

He passionately told me about the song he was recording the next day at a nearby studio and repeatedly told me that I had to be there. Well aware that our souls are old mates, it was no accident that we were meeting up—as the dream from the night before had already informed me. It was now gut wrenchingly confirmed. *I wish I didn't feel behind—I have to be brave like him and put myself out there.*

Right before we said good-bye, Alex reminded me again to be at the recording studio the next day. Then I zipped off to a coffee shop to start writing.

Later that night, I sent him a message to let him know that I would be around that evening if he wanted to meet up again. *Oh, well, if not tonight, then for sure tomorrow. That's going to be so much fun!*

Then at the exact moment that I was opening the door to a Korean restaurant to dine alone, my phone rang. It was Alex, and he told me that his friend had suggested going to a Korean spa downtown. He then asked if I wanted to join.

At first I thought he was kidding, but then he told me he would text me the address. *Well, that was crazy timing!*

When I got there, he was with two friends sitting on pillows on the floor waiting for sushi. He was scheduled for a massage and told me that I should go with his one friend to get a treatment. So I scheduled a fifteen-dollar full-body scrub with her, which was an unfamiliar treatment to me. It sounded relaxing.

Little did I know what I was getting into. An older woman started splashing me with buckets of water and began aggressively scrubbing me. She kept abruptly flipping me over and blasting me with more water. My reaction was laughter, while praying on the inside for it to be over. *I feel like an animal getting a bath. I guess relaxation is not the end goal for this treatment.*

Afterward, we all bounced around from the red clay room, the wood charcoal room, the ice room, and the salt room. At one point, Alex and I were sitting in what I can only describe as the inside of a large refrigerator, and I just sat there not really knowing what to say—I was just deliriously tired.

At that moment, I realized that we were going from room to room with his friends, surrounded by Asian people. I had just been uncomfortably exposed and humiliated. It was the dream I had the night before. *What is going on? What in the world is all this? Thank goodness I documented that!*

The next morning, we met at the recording studio, and the room was filled with passion and raw talent. There were solo vocalists and a choir group that had worked with many musical talents, like Michael Jackson, Madonna, and Aloe Black. They repeatedly sent chills up my spine.

Everyone kept hugging each other, and it was sheer magic watching Alex orchestrate the group. His artistic ability to turn his vision into reality inspired me in a deep way—it was genius. I had tears in my eyes.

They were working on the song "Come Home," and I just watched in amazement as a group of old souls passionately worked together on such a moving piece. It was an absolute honor to be there. His energy was contagious. When we parted ways, he smiled and told me that he couldn't wait to read my book. The pressure was on, but in an extremely supportive way.

After the Antix encounter, I saw Ashley again, and we went to a spiritual sanctuary to meet more people who imparted powerful wisdom and perspective. We were lost in a spiritual bubble I can't begin to explain.

48

PAY IT FORWARD, BABY

There was no denying that my lifestyle was wearing me down. I was flashing in between what I wanted my life to be and my physical reality where I wasn't happy with my work, my relationships, or my living situation. I was so lonely.

I kept moving like Dawn predicted, and I longed for the happy ending in Northern California she had described. But an odd force was holding me where I was and yanking me around into the most random situations.

I couldn't find my place, and so many strange energetic things were happening. I existed in the static place between stations, and I ached for clarity and to be in complete alignment with my vision. The story lines were confusing me, and the writer's block was now torturing me again. There were no responses from the publishing houses, and Mike wasn't holding up his end of the contract now that the TV show was officially not happening.

Things turned especially sour. I couldn't grasp it.

On top of that, I couldn't ignore the homeless people that I kept seeing in my area. They had such a unique perspective on life and eye-opening stories. Many were educated, had traveled extensively, and were artists, veterans, or former working professionals. When I would ask to hear their stories, they would frequently say, "It's nice to talk to someone." My heart was bleeding.

I was driving by some people a couple of times a day, and it was impossible to not talk to them. I would bring them basic supplies, clothes, a hot meal, or whatever I could do. I quickly became too attached and overextended myself. I wanted to give everything yet had close to nothing. In retrospect, I was circling the drain myself, so I related to them. They were people, not homeless people, just people. I felt their souls, and it was breaking me.

As I was intentionally paying it forward, a friend of mine gave me a guest pass to use at a local clubhouse. So I went alone one sunny afternoon to clear my head and decompress. There was hardly anyone there, so I sprawled out in the hot tub, closed my eyes, and gave gratitude for the warm sun on my face.

Within moments, a woman came in, and we ended up talking about writing and where I was with anxiously waiting on the publishing world. Without me saying anything else, she excitedly said, "You know who you have to meet? Catherine Ryan Hyde." I had no idea who that was, but she adamantly insisted that I reach out to her. She then told me that she was the author of *Pay It Forward*, and my body nudged me with reassurance.

So, shortly afterward, I contacted her, and we made plans to meet for coffee. It took a while for our schedules to line up, but when we did get together, she gave me excellent advice and explained the publishing world in greater depth. The timing was cosmic.

She then offered to interview me once the book was done. *Yes, awesome! It certainly pays to pay it forward! I can't wait to get to the marketing of this book! That's the fun part, especially with what I have planned!*

49

CUE THE NFL

It had been months since I had last spoken with him, so it was shocking to see the e-mail. It was from the former NFL player I had spoken on the phone with about consciousness. To my surprise, he was asking if it was too late to meet up. *Wow, didn't expect to hear from this guy again.*

So I wrote him back and asked if he was coming to California in the near future. Sure enough, he was heading out to San Diego in a few weeks, and we made plans to get together. *This is so random!*

Just a couple days later, I was out writing when I tapped into another old mate of mine. There was an awareness that he was about to sit down next to me. *Now who is this?*

Sure enough, a man sat down next to me, and I just continued my work as I started to read his energy. He was extremely focused on the football game, and he asked me if I was into it. I smiled and told him that it's not my thing—just before he told me his son played in the NFL. *Ha, what's with the football theme? I know I didn't set intentions on that. Can we manifest a dance theme? You got my order wrong.*

After speaking for a while, I decided to ask him what he knew about this Ricky character. A passionate rant poured out of Sam's mouth, but not about his football career. Instead, he was mostly talking about his involvement in Access Consciousness, holistic healing, and his courage to walk away from so much money to do what he loved.

At this point, I closed the computer, and we dove into a deep conversation and couldn't stop exchanging information, as small talk didn't even occur to us.

Sam was a brilliant man and had unbelievable stories of traveling the world with his dad, who had been in the public eye. I didn't ask who he was. It didn't matter. I ended up telling him that I was meeting up with Ricky, and we made plans to meet up in San Diego when I was down there for that. I thanked him for the conversation, and he gave me his contact information.

I soon realized that he was the son of one of the artists on my Pandora list, Solomon Burke. *Wow, that was really special. We have to make sure we honor soulful music legends—they're the heart of history. They were singing the truth. Okay, Law of Attraction, keep the old souls coming my way!*

Right before San Diego, I used a free voucher I had to book a hotel in a less-congested part of the city. When I called Expedia to use the points that I had accumulated, they told me that the hotel was booked for that night. The representative mentioned one up the road, and I booked it. It didn't matter where I was staying.

◊

Upon arrival a couple days later, I went to check in, and the desk clerk said, "Are you here for Access Consciousness?" *Umm, what? How do you know that? Seriously, how do you know that?*

My eyes suspiciously darted around, thinking that maybe Ricky was somehow there—as impractical as that thought was. *Okay, I'm confused!*

He told me that this was the hotel that was holding the conference for Access Consciousness. *With all the hotels in this area, what are the chances that I'm staying at the one for his consciousness program? Wow, these coincidences will always blow my mind!* It was quite obvious I was supposed to be there.

I met up with Sam and a friend of his who had played with Solomon Burke. We were time warping through history as they told personal stories about music legends and revealed inside truths about their lives.

It made me think about how history is altered depending on the source that is trying to portray people and events a certain way. *We should be questioning everything, as the truth is so often buried. Humans are fallible, and power and fame corrupt.*

50

OPEN-MIND SURGERY

It will always baffle me how much and how quickly I related to Ricky Williams, not that he wasn't intimidating at first. Luckily, he was down to earth so my silly side came out right away. Before I knew it, we were high-fiving during a passionate talk about higher consciousness.

Ricky reframed my thinking on some major limiting beliefs that were holding me back and brought awareness to some blind spots. There were fireworks "…of aha moments for me."

Obviously, many people have stereotyped him, but it's safe to say that he's one of the most brilliant people I've encountered. I thanked him for the "open-mind surgery" that he had just performed, which is what I call it when someone clears out maladaptive beliefs and helps me evolve my thinking.

The next day, he sent me a text and invited me to breakfast so that we could talk some more. He told me that I was a more powerful creator than I was aware of and to use him as a resource. He offered to help me in any way he could, but I had no idea what kind of help I needed. I even told him I wasn't ready; we both had that awareness. My vision was still blurry and my life was very tangled. I was still in the tornado.

His energy field had shifted me, though, and I knew I would reach out when I was *ready. That was intense. What a cool character in this wacky movie. I needed that! Ha, I asked for help!*

It was about a month later, and I couldn't remember what team Ricky had played for, my lack of interest in football remaining intact. When I looked it up, I found something else—a video about Ricky's social anxiety disorder.

He spoke about keeping a helmet on during interviews and how that had been a very controversial thing. *What? He suffered from that too? I have always wanted to keep a hat on in social situations to help with my anxiety! Why would people worry about him having a helmet on? What's the big deal? I bet he has felt completely alienated like I always have, despite the unceasing social stimulation.*

There was something about Ricky's story that gave me the courage to continue plowing through my anxiety disorder. *I know I will end up speaking in public, so I need to figure this out! Figure something out. Get yourself in front of people. Do it now! You have to get ready!*

Knowing that public speaking groups weren't for me, I hightailed it to the beach and decided that for the first time, I would dance in front of people the way that I do when I'm alone. Despite my nervousness, the dance exploded out of me. The people vanished, and my free spirit only saw the ocean. *Ahh, that's the trick—I need to just focus on what I'm passionate about.*

To my surprise, young kids actually started joining me, and people were asking me if I was a choreographer. Some people even told me that I should go on *So You Think You Can Dance*, and I even got a round of applause. I just laughed and was grateful for the positive feedback. *Hmm, my pain is definitely translating into dance. Wow, people seem to like it. Maybe I'm not crazy to think that dance is part of my mission. Thanks for the push, Ricky!*

51

A FLASH OF ANTIX

Shortly afterward, Antix reached out, and we made plans to meet up in L.A. again—of course. We met at a chill restaurant, and I got there early to do some writing. I was feeling really off, but his energy blasted me instantly, and we picked up where we'd left off. *Ahh, how do I do what you do? How do I make this all happen?*

A friend of his joined shortly afterward. We sat down for some omelets, and he inquired about the progress of the book. It was disheartening to explain that I had recently gone through the publishing process but had heard nothing.

My body wanted to break down and sob and tell him that I thought I would have great news at this point. I wanted to pour my heart out but just couldn't. I had been so confident in the direction things seemed to be going, disappointment was inevitable.

The book was in limbo, and the story was confusing me. *Ugh, I'm sorry—I feel behind. I can't figure out how to get this book out there in the best way. It's overwhelming and the characters are so random. I'm so lost, and I'm desperate for the happy ending that was predicted.*

Without a moment's delay, Alex normalized my experience and said a sentence so imperative that I just quietly nodded: "Take your time and do it right." It was the exact thing that I needed to hear in order to release some of the self-imposed pressure.

A deep breath helped as clarity rushed in. It became clear that despite my eagerness to get my messages out to the world, it was more important that I deliver them accurately. *Okay, I really needed that.*

From there we went to the beach and listened to music. It was the perfect scenario to ask the questions that I had prepared. However, I couldn't even speak intelligently. It wasn't that I was nervous around him; I just couldn't communicate. He even asked me what other rappers I was into, and I really couldn't name any, despite the long list of artists I listen to. It was stupidly frustrating and even more embarrassing.

I knew spirits were messing with me. I had so much to say but couldn't. I wanted to open up to him about the darkness that was so obviously trying to stop me. In that moment though, I was the Tin Man from *The Wizard of Oz*. It was another stolen experience. *Ahh, I don't feel like myself! Something is messing with me!*

I met up with Sam later that day. One minute I was fine, and the next I went brain-dead. I was childlike and helpless even though earlier we had been laughing and lost in conversation. It was such an obvious attack, and it was the breaking point for me. I decided not to venture to L.A. for a long time.

52

I ATE DIRT—LITERALLY

Shortly afterward, I received another e-mail from OWN after not getting one for quite some time. This one was about the writer's workshop in Maui with Wayne Dyer, Doreen Virtue, and several other people from the publishing house I had my eye on.

"You're going to Maui."

What? I can't afford that right now. Who would I go with? Nope, sorry, Universe, this isn't a good time. Remember, I'm the struggling writer who is trying to keep up with these storylines—trying not to starve.

"You're going to Maui."

At that exact moment, the trip I won to Maui popped in my head. *Ha, was that foreshadowing? Universe, if you want me to go, then please give me a sign. Otherwise, I'm just focusing on the hours of editing ahead of me because I want that behind me. I want out of this puzzle.*

For a few days, I played the cognitive dissonance game. Should I go? Or should I play it safe? Back and forth I went. Until one day, a reminder to think from my heart, not my head, flashed in my mind. There it was. The answer I had been searching for.

My heart began thumping with joy, and my soul was halfway to the island already. There was nothing but intense love coming out of this decision; the energy made me giddy. The somatic markers confirmed it. *Wow, I'm going to Maui—but how? I can't afford this right now. Thank you for making this happen!*

That day at work, I told my friends I was going to Maui, despite not knowing how that was going to happen. There was just such a strong feeling. I spent the whole day dreaming about what the conference would be like and what I would say to Wayne and Doreen. I couldn't wait.

However, that night was destined for an epic curveball—one I had sensed my whole life. It was the first time I had ever overcorrected and lost control of my car. It happened so fast. It rolled over four lanes, and I came within an inch of losing my life. A distorted version of me climbed out of the driver's side of the upside-down car. It was all an out-of-body experience, like a lucid dream. The prediction of a lower spinal injury now made sense.

When I saw my car in daylight the next morning, it became even more perplexing that I was walking. The men who towed my car couldn't figure out how I had survived either. It was totaled, and they said that if the car had slid just a tiny bit more, it would have been the end for me. The words echoed within. Every cell in my body was reactively spazzing.

As predicted, I had just moved, so the car was filled with six boxes of books. When I opened the door to start pulling them out, I couldn't believe what I saw. Every box was still completely closed up, and only one book had mysteriously escaped—*The Secret*. It was propped upright in the back seat as if someone had carefully placed it there. A chill shot up my spine. *Oh, let me guess, it's important to realize that I attracted the accident? Not now, Universe! Not now!*

My other possessions were scattered throughout the car—including my laptop, which had flown out of the car. There was a thick layer of dirt and glass covering the keyboard. I frantically tried to clean it up and was shocked that it turned on.

Somehow everything was in there, and not a single thing was destroyed. There wasn't even a scratch. It made absolutely no sense. *How did I survive this? How are all my things intact? How can I move but fireworks are exploding within me? I can't believe I'm alive—well, sort of alive. What is this new energy buried deep within me?*

A GHOST

This was my first car accident, so I wasn't prepared for the agonizing fear of driving that transpired. It didn't take much to reset the trauma. A loud noise alone vibrated within like a turbulent plane. Driving by car accidents caused me to hyperventilate.

This was the car accident I had sensed most of my life—I had always said, "One day I will be in a horrible accident, but I survive." I had survived physically, but internally I was spinning.

The adrenaline lasted for days, and the night terrors started instantly, leaving me drenched in sweat on a regular basis. The sleep deprivation wasn't helping. *Just relax. You're in shock.*

There was so much pressure to figure everything out, and looking back, the process was just a blurred haze. I could barely remember who I was or who others were. Nothing seemed real. I was just lifeless.

Even though I continued to smile and hide my torment, I knew it wasn't me with the reins anymore. Everything had shut down. *Wow, I shouldn't be making decisions in this state. I just want it all behind me. I don't care anymore. Everything is so heavy.*

My spirit was broken, and it was almost impossible to keep caring. I didn't need a setback of that caliber when I had already been burnt out for so long. My heart ached for some relief.

Everything was pitch black again. It was beyond disorienting, and I knew I was under possession, and there was nothing I could do about it. Something else was operating my body, parading me around, behaving and speaking for me, violating me in an unrelenting way.

You never think something as dramatic as possession can happen to you, at least I didn't. This is a tangent I will refrain from delving into more because these stories will be better told on stage. As unbearable as it was, I decided to focus my intention on miracles coming out of this experience and attempted to regain my life.

54

THE HEALING CREW

My arm was numb, my tailbone was injured, my hip was torqued, and the electrical zaps from the nerve damage were relentless. There were also shooting pains, tingling sensations, and constant dizziness. There was very obvious memory damage as well from cracking my head on the window. I was like Dory from the movie *Finding Nemo*. My life had spiraled out of control, and I was grasping at straws to put it back together.

My mind, however, was playing tricks on me. Several times I would think that I was chewing on dirt and glass like I had after the accident. The ground was no longer a stable surface as my stomach did cartwheels. It would often feel like I was being shoved when no one was there at all. Everything was out of sorts. Everything startled me. Everything was running on autopilot.

Luckily, the first blessing was that I had stopped seeing Ms. Erika, my acupuncturist, for financial reasons, and now the insurance from the accident meant we would be meeting regularly. She was able to help with physical relief, but the emotional trauma was clearly going to take a long time, especially with the denial at play.

She introduced me to a chiropractor named Dr. Rob Gottesman, who used an approach called the directional non-force technique, which uses the body's intelligence to realign itself without any force. His technique addressed other physical issues that surfaced as well. It was fascinatingly more complex than I could comprehend, but the healing results were undeniable.

I worked with a hypnotherapist and a Hawaiian healer as well. The accident had to be deeply relived during this time, as trapped energy was released. We worked to reframe the incident and to manage the pain. I was compartmentalizing it so that I could move on with my life. This wasn't an easy process.

It was like the energy-healing SWAT team showed up to put my humpty dumpty self back together. But through everything, my tears remained trapped. *When can I have my body back? When can I dance the pain away? Will I ever be able to dance at the level I was at? What is this new, powerful energy buried within me? How will I ever be able to let it out?*

My hypnotherapist tried to get my tears to budge, but they remained stuck. He also told me that I had become addicted to learning but that it was time for me to become a teacher. He repeatedly told me it was time to get on stage. So in addition to helping me cope with the trauma from the accident, he was also restructuring my subconscious mind to prepare me for public speaking. Even in the thick haze, my eye was still on delivering my messages.

There was no denying that I had undergone a radical personality change. I had bursts of anger and other unreasonable behaviors. Any form of transition sent my brain blasting off into a foggy space, and I knew I would never be the same. I even wondered if my trancelike existence was going to be a permanent state.

At my wit's end of being tortured in my mind, I grabbed my *Diagnostic and Statistical Manual of Mental Disorders* and looked up the criteria for post-traumatic stress disorder (PTSD). My head nodded slowly as I began checking off the matching symptoms. I decided that I was going to use energy to heal and then help others in the future. I officially knew I wanted to get into holistic energy healing to help people relieve their suffering. I just wasn't sure how to make that happen.

Meanwhile, I had to start completely over. The most basic things were a struggle, as I had to relearn things I had done most of my life. Outside of work and healing, I cut myself off from just about everyone.

$\Diamond$

Then my family came out to visit me, and that should have been a relaxing and healing time for me. However, we were attacked aggressively again. Dark spirits circled the building, we saw dark wispy shadows in the water as the heated pool turned ice cold in an instant, the TV turned on by itself, and my sidewalk was so bright it illogically blinded us, considering it was cloudy and had never happened before—or after.

We were exhausted for no reason, unable to meet my friends, and couldn't do many of the activities I had planned. We never once used the heated pool with a waterslide, which was the whole point of renting that airbnb. So many things happened that made no rational sense, and it was all just one blurred haze of a visit. Then at the exact moment they left, things snapped back to *normal.*

I grieved for weeks, just pinned down in bed. Satan was having a field day, thrashing me around like a rag doll. *There is no point in living if I can't be with my family and closest friends. I want control over my life again! I can't do this anymore. Leave me alone!*

As everything spun around me, it was always at my lowest moment when I would randomly hear Antix's song "Come Home," the song from the recording studio. The exact lines that would reel me in were "Stare those demons in the eye" and "It's the fight of your life." That song was saving my life. *Don't give up. Pick yourself up. Think about what other people have survived. Follow the light. Get through this, and get others through it!*

55

PSYCHIC TO PSYCHIC

There was still faith that this was a blessing in disguise, as the purpose of the accident continued to become clearer. There was a flicker of light at the end of the tunnel.

Somehow the insurance money ended up being more than double the amount the car was worth. *Well, technically, there's the money for Maui, but I don't even want to go. Maybe I should have clarified that I wanted it to show up in a non-traumatic way. I would need a clear sign to go because I'm a mess. I know it's part of my journey, but I'm so heavy.*

A few weeks prior, Stephanie told me that she had a session with an energy reader and that he mentioned me several times. This wasn't the first time we had come up in each other's readings; this time it was just more obvious.

"Get a reading from Justin."

This phrase had been surfacing many times since Stephanie told me about her reading. If he had tapped into me that accurately through her, I couldn't help but be curious about what he would say to me. I ached for a strong message. For weeks I just let that thought go, but it relentlessly surfaced. *Okay, fine. Let's see what he has to say.*

The first thing he commented on was that I was going on a big trip and to not second-guess myself. Justin then said, "Do you know what Hawaii is? I like Hawaii for you. Pay attention to Hawaii; you find so much peace there. Things make sense for you there, and it is a spiritual trip for you." *Uhh, well I guess that clears that up.*

He then firmly stated that I had a three-month writing boot camp and that I would be moving and have a new life at the end of the summer. He said the final chapters hadn't happened yet and to pay attention to the ending. His exact line was, "It's blood, sweat, and tears time." He predicted that the next two years were going to be hectic.

Justin then stated that I write and that I have a story to share. He told me that writing is therapeutic for me and that he was seeing book signings. He encouraged me to keep writing at night and to keep reading a book by Dale. Sure enough, a Dale Carnegie book was sitting next to me on my bed as he said that.

He told me that I sleep alone and it made him sad. He commented on the fact that I'm lonely and that I need love and to come out of hibernation. *But I'm in my writing cave. I don't have time. I'm so sick of hearing that. I have nothing to give someone else right now. I'm barely surviving.*

He proceeded to tell me that a man was coming into my life who is also connected with writing and to be open to him. I was shocked when he mentioned that my spine was currently jacked. He said it is bumping me in a new direction. He then specifically mentioned my tailbone and said that everything happens for a reason, but it will take more time to understand.

He predicted me buying a house within a year or two, being in a significant relationship, getting a dog, and traveling a lot to help people. It was all very familiar. He also mentioned doing workshops and teaching people in groups. He firmly stated that I needed to be teaching.

Justin continued to inform me that I needed to learn how to run energy through my body and hands—specifically Reiki healing. He told me that love and money couldn't come in until I worked through my blocks. He said that I was calling him to understand my gift more and that I need to take a class or a workshop to further develop my healing abilities. From there, Justin said, "You're so empathic," and that I needed to not be so scared of my gift. He predicted that I was going to make some new connections and would end up working from a shop giving readings.

He then got very serious and said, "You're psychic. You read people all the time. You need to learn how to trust yourself, and you can do what I do. You're a medium, and you can earn money doing this." *Uhh, what? I'm too scared to do that.*

He recommended hypnosis and said that it was for clearing channels for more clear writing. Just like my hypnotherapist, he said, "You need to speak in front of people, and when you do, the world is yours. That's when it all opens up." *How, though? It's like this isn't even my choice—it's a total mystery to me! I swear my mind is about to implode.*

He told me that I have a very deep connection to Jim Morrison's soul and that we have a similar purpose with our channeled writing. Hawaii came up again, and he said that it was very important for me to surrender to spirit. He mentioned traditions of forgiveness like *Ho'opono'pono.*

He then referenced Rosie the Riveter, the strong female icon from World War II. He said that I needed to flex my wings and start to fly and to be a warrior like her. *Umm, no pressure. I guess*

I'm going to Maui! That was definitely an obvious sign. The trip was booked with not much time to spare—my guardian angels were thrilled.

56

MAGICAL MAUI

Upon arriving in Maui, a sense of home greeted me—even through the thick fog I was in. There was no denying that a circle of darkness was weighing me down. I kept calling home and saying, "Something is wrong. I don't feel right."

Mysteriously oversized black blisters formed on the bottom of my feet out of nowhere, and I could barely walk. The strangest things were happening. *Something* was messing with me. It didn't want me to attract what was on that island.

However, as soon as I slipped into the green water, my energy shifted. The sobbing began instantly. The tears that had been trapped for more than three months suddenly escaped. The residual effects from the accident were exiting my body at the exact time that I needed to be in the highest vibration possible.

It took a few days, but I centered myself to the best of my ability. I arrived at the hotel three hours before the event and wandered around among the whirlwind of people. I had no expectations or itinerary. I was out by the ocean when my gut nudged me toward two women who were off to the side talking. So I approached them and asked if they were part of the writer's conference. They both nodded yes. *Ha, of course.*

They asked if I was part of the social media group, but of course I was not. I learned that one of the women had started a Maui 2015 Facebook page and that about fifty people attending the event had been communicating with each other for months. They had made plans to meet at 4:30 for dinner before the event.

Before I knew it, we were the epicenter of a swarm of soulful writers. There was one woman that I clicked with right away, Jackie. We all exchanged beautiful stories, many of which entailed a back-and-forth decision process of whether to attend the event in the first place. I didn't share the fact that a near-death experience had been the catalyst for me.

Many of us had powerful and dramatic stories about the Universe pushing us to attend the conference. *Wow, it's because of the accident that I'm here with my kind of people. Look at that; no social media required for this gal!*

Many women talked about meeting their twin flames, who share a more intense connection than soul mates. As they did, chills kept blasting up my spine. I had talked about wanting to date "my male twin" my whole life; I had been extremely tapped into him. As much as I ached to meet him, I had been pushing him away for so long. I was only a fragment of myself.

The first night of the event featured Doreen Virtue, who is an angel expert and an absolute blessing for this world. The energy was making the room pulsate. *Wow, I'm actually here. I have to talk to her at some point. I can't wait to see Wayne speak tomorrow and to finally talk to him—with a voice this time!*

◊

The next day, I arrived at the conference and was sitting alone, enjoying my breakfast and coffee. Then my inner voice spoke up.

"Go out to the lobby."

Really? I'm pretty content where I am. However, I sprang up and went to the lobby for no apparent reason. Who did I run into first? That's right, Mr. Wayne Dyer.

That's when I noticed who was next to him: the friend I had made, Jackie. They were about to take a picture, so I smiled and offered to take it for them. I had so much to say to Wayne, but there was a fierce energy block. I didn't even say hello or get a picture with him. How crazy is that? There was that same wild magnetic pull, but something—the impenetrable wall—was stopping me from approaching him.

This wasn't just true for Wayne. I never spoke to Doreen either, despite them both being within arm's reach. At one point, she was sitting by herself right near me, and all I wanted to do was to sit next to her and strike up a conversation and share a story or two. I really can't think of someone more fitting for my spiritual journey. It was a blessing that I couldn't pursue, despite the fact that I had just flown that far to make it happen. My eyes were bugged out in frustration.

I commanded my body to go over there, but it wouldn't. There was no anxiety, and it was the perfect opportunity to receive a powerful message. It was worse than the Tin Man from *The Wizard of Oz.* The wall was up between us, and eventually I had to leave because it was so unbearable. *I'm losing it! This is so disorienting!*

During the conference the next few days, Wayne repeatedly said, "What I need to do requires me to be alone." He explained that he had to spend most of his time alone and that he needed silence. Every cell of my being resonated with that. *That's all I need too! No one gets that, though, and they take it personally. The silence is the truth!*

He also kept saying, "Writing is about letting go and not caring about the outcome." The more I watched him, the more I ached to do what he did.

We shifted gears into a short break. Since no one was standing on the stage, I walked to the front of the room to get a feel for the bright lights in front of a crowd of people. It was at this exact moment that I realized I wasn't afraid to speak in public anymore. *Hmm, I can do this. I actually can't wait to do this! I want to do what Wayne does. Period!*

I then walked past the lobby and kept marching toward one of the farthest points of the property to avoid the rush of people. As I opened the door, I almost took out a petite woman as she was exiting. We both smiled and apologized profusely.

When I was heading back to the conference, these words popped into my mind: "Wayne and I are nothing more than magnets."

At that very instant, I glanced up to see Wayne and the woman I almost collided with talking and powerwalking by me, away from the conference. The only people around were the three of us, and I still didn't even say hello. *This is so ridiculous.*

The conference continued, and I kept passing by Wayne, but I still did not interact with him directly, even though everyone else was. *Why can't I talk to him and Doreen like I need to? I didn't come all the way here to not get answers. Something is seriously wrong...*

57

GREETINGS FROM DAVID

That night, I walked into Lahaina to clear my head and stroll around the art galleries. Just a short distance into the walk, an older man with a big white beard stopped and moved out of my way to let me pass by first. He had been pushing a shopping cart with his possessions in there. He immediately said, "Hi," and flashed me a genuine smile.

Many people would have ignored him or vaguely reciprocated the greeting. We instantly started talking, and he began making local recommendations of things for me to do. He told me his name was David, and he kept repeating, "It's a good day." His aura was warm and kind. His energy field was saint-like.

We then parted ways and walked in opposite directions. As I walked by the Hard Rock Cafe, I heard, *"You're going there,"* from within. I knew it would be with someone else too, but with whom was a complete mystery. So for the next couple hours, I gazed at stunning artwork and watched the sunset. Now away from the conference, I felt more like myself again.

I sat on the wall across the street from the Hard Rock Cafe and still had a feeling that I was going to have dinner there with someone. However, I wasn't interacting with anyone at all. So I just sat there puzzled with my headphones in.

David popped in my head, and at that exact moment I saw him coming up the street. So I waved to him and walked toward him. I offered to buy him dinner, and within no time we were sitting at the Hard Rock Cafe—his suggestion.

Hours passed by as we talked about mutual perspectives, shared passions, and many genres of music. He had attended Berkeley College, been involved in politics, moved around a lot, and carried with him an undeniably fine-tuned vocabulary. Now he was homeless.

We continued to talk about world issues, especially how people are living in fear and working against each other. David explained that he cleaned up the beaches frequently with friends. We discussed the power of paying it forward. He was awake. He was cultured. He was brilliant. His eyes were soft, and when he spoke there was truth; it was resonating with me. It was an honor to be listening to him. My instinct was respect.

At one point, David said that he wished people would have bumper stickers on their cars that said, "Thou shall not litter. It's a missing commandment." I asked David what he wished people would change, and he replied, "I wish I could teach people not to think so much, in a Buddhist way, of course." From there we delved into a conversation about Confucianism.

What was surprising was that the whole staff at the restaurant knew who he was. They kept coming up to our table to talk to him, and it was clear that they all genuinely liked him. They even came over with a painting and said that they had been holding it for him. We continued to exchange many laughs. He was a familiar soul—and my mates come in all shapes and sizes.

David kept saying things like, "You're nice," "Life is amazing," "Imagine what other people are going through," and "Thanks for being my friend; it made my day." That made my day!

It was heartbreaking to leave beautiful Maui, but I parted ways feeling rewired, with a sense that things would open up. A miraculous healing had occurred there. Even though an evil force had hindered me from talking to the people I needed to, I had found my peace again. I was so grateful, but I also couldn't fathom how I was leaving that island without having connected with the two angelic souls I had been magnetized to in the first place. I didn't even get to look Wayne in the eyes, his healing eyes.

When I got home and entered my room, the one angel figurine that I owned was shattered all over the floor. There had been several books on my mantel but none had ever fallen over. Until then, that is.

Ironically, the book that had knocked it over was Wayne Dyer's book *The Power of Intention*. With a chill in my spine, there was an ominous energy that was laughing in my face.

58

THE MAUI AFTERMATH

Now in a higher vibration, everything shifted quickly. There was a newfound energy pumping through me. The accident was somehow yanking me forward—well, dragging me forward. For the first time in years, there was an inner, magnetic pull toward Northern California.

What shocked me the most was that my cystic acne miraculously faded away the second I returned from Maui. The anxiety decreased in suit. It was the first relief I had in almost twenty years, and just like that, I was released from a physical imprisonment that had formerly appeared to be a life sentence. *Wow, this is how other people have always felt? I finally feel free in my body. I can't believe this! This is the answer to my prayers! I have ached for this most of my life! Thank you! Thank you! Thank you! What is my direction now? It's as though my life just started!*

Then out of nowhere, I heard from Ms. Lisa from the leadership organization. It had been almost a year since she had reached out. She had felt blocked for so long.

We finally connected on the phone. She apologized for not getting back to me sooner and explained that I had recently popped into her head. We both agreed it was all about timing.

She had me send her a headshot, biography, and sample chapters. Over the next couple of weeks, I anxiously waited to hear from her. The pull to Northern California became stronger, but there was no plan.

Shortly afterward, I was sitting in my parked car about to work out on the beach when I had a feeling to check something online. When I did, all I saw was an announcement that Dr. Wayne Dyer had passed away.

A flood of emotion blasted my heart, and tears trolled down my face. *The world just lost a beautiful soul—and I never told him what I wanted to.*

Before I could process anything, my car suddenly jerked as I heard a loud bang. I looked up to see that a Jeep Wrangler had backed up into my parked car, despite the fact that the passenger was out of the car assisting in the parking job. When I got out of the car, I remained calm when I saw the indent in the hood of my new car. *Really? Another car accident?*

The two guys who had hit me were really nice, and we ended up laughing the whole thing off and decided to hang out sometime. They then told me that they work for KSBY, the local radio station. *Hmm, that's interesting. The marketing for this book just seems to blast into my life. Everything happens for a reason! Thanks, Wayne!*

Afterward, I took a walk on the beach and could feel Wayne with me very strongly. I asked him to stay by my side and to help me finish the book and get on stage to teach. I was grieving the loss of my role model. I told him that I was tired of messing up my story and allowing fear to control me. I begged for protection. I then held my hand up to give him the *pen*. My book was now in his hands.

I just happened to have an appointment with Ms. Erika scheduled the next morning, and when I went to see her, she said that she could feel Wayne too. She said that he was holding my hand and that I had not missed anything in Maui—which had been the question I had asked many times since that trip. We proceeded to have the most intense session yet.

A few days later, Erika told me that Wayne was continuing to visit her, and she commented on his beautiful soul. The whole experience was completely overwhelming, but it confirmed what I already knew: Wayne was going to guide me toward my dreams, and he was now one of my spirit guides.

At this time, my gut encouraged me to quit my job, pack up my possessions in preparation for a move back to Northern California, and to head to the East Coast to edit and spend time with my family beforehand. So I followed the inner instructions, despite the fact that nothing had officially pulled me back up there.

When I got back to the East Coast, I heard from Ms. Lisa again. She gave me very positive feedback and asked me to come out to meet her in person. She told me that I could stay with her when I returned to California. There it was, the official pull back up north. The final chapters were going to be right back where I started, exactly where Dawn predicted.

I quickly caught the book up to the present times, and when I compared it to the original e-book that I had written, I was shocked at the transformation in my writing. I was actually humiliated by my original writing. *Wow, what a long, crazy journey this was! I'm so happy I didn't try to sell that piece. It's not ready. I can make it so much better! This is it, the final stretch.*

59

GUIDANCE FROM WAYNE

My instincts were forcing me to venture out farther on a limb. I flew out to San Francisco, and Ms. Lisa and I spent a few days together getting to know each other. We went to the core leadership class, and she called me up to speak about the Law of Attraction.

There it was, the moment that I had equally dreaded and ached for. It only took a moment to grasp how much I loved talking about something I was so passionate about. Awareness that I needed to get as much practice in as possible excited me. In fact, I was hooked!

Afterward, I watched the other speakers, who were nothing short of powerhouses. There was one woman in particular whom I had noticed nodding her head up and down in agreement when I was speaking. During her presentation, I realized how much her messages were in alignment with my book.

As I sat there proudly sponging in the moment, she approached me. She gave me some great advice, and she said that I reminded her of another speaker, and author, who was going to be presenting in about a week at a different college. She then invited me to attend.

It was clear that major connections and support were flying in. The pull to Northern California was beginning to make sense—but it was still blurry.

As soon as I arrived in Sonoma, the momentum picked up. I met up with someone that I hadn't seen in almost two years, Hank. After speaking with him for a while, I learned that he did the printing for Hay House, meaning Wayne Dyer's printing. *Ha, of course! Well, I guess I found which printer to use—thanks, Wayne! Of course it's in Sonoma, right where I started.*

Right before I walked out, Hank asked if I got a copy of Wayne's last book, *Remembering Heaven*. He told me that it came in that day, and he handed me a copy. Hank then said, "Now if you can just get a medium, you could ask him how heaven is." *Or I could just ask him myself.*

I just smirked. He had no idea how big of a role Wayne was playing in my journey. *Ha, if he only knew the irony of that!*

60

DEAD WEIGHT

The leadership program at the college was amazing, and I wasn't nervous while speaking at all. At the end of the conference, Peter, the author, approached me. He handed me a business card and asked if I wanted to meet up at some point. The somatic markers within confirmed I was on the right track.

I then attended another core leadership workshop and spoke again, this time about vision boards. There was an eagerness to become great at this and do this at a larger scale—a much larger scale.

The next time I saw Peter, he strongly encouraged me to reach out to a friend of his, Monica.

When she and I met we hit it off immediately, and we quickly knew we were meant to have a voice together. The irony of it all was that she lived in Sonoma, just a matter of blocks from where I was staying. I was still in a fog and could feel dark spirits all around me, but my gut was exploding with positive reinforcement. I was being magnetized toward the happy ending that Dawn had predicted.

Unfortunately, at this time I was pushed over the edge when my PTSD was severely triggered. It was like falling off a mountain. Even the physical sensations of the accident returned. I was a spinning mess. Any transition was almost impossible, and I couldn't comprehend what was happening around me.

I kept trying to follow the storylines, but when I went to the leadership programs, I was noticeably not myself. I was now sitting off to the side and shrinking in the back, unable to socialize or focus.

I had gone from speaking and wearing business suits to hiding in the back in a sweatshirt. It was unbearable. I wanted to be there so badly but was just too disoriented. I had to keep leaving, as I was in the trance state, unable to express myself. I was back to watching my life as an out-of-body experience, the reigns not in my hands.

Dark spirits were doing everything they could to stop me from moving forward. *They* had latched on aggressively and did an award-winning job at humiliating me. I mean, we're talking about dark entities; what do you think they were doing with me? They certainly weren't braiding my hair.

On top of that, I was doing everything wrong to suppress my pain. I was too disoriented to be making logical decisions. My fear was winning. My vices were winning. I was losing. Big time.

I was at my wit's end and was just about to move back to the East Coast in a moment of sheer exhaustion, anguish, and zero hope. I was defeated. I was now the starving artist, and I didn't know how to tell anyone just how bad it was. I did my best to appear normal, in vain of course. I was in full panic mode.

As I got down to the final hours, a job finally came in—in

Sonoma, of course. I had applied to jobs all over Northern California and wanted to live somewhere new. There was one coastal area that I had discovered on my drive up that I had fallen in love with and wanted to settle down in. I had named it Zen Island—and that's where my heart was. But it was as though I didn't have a choice. All arrows were pointing at Sonoma.

At this time, Hank told me about an up-and-coming innovative thinker who had created a program that was going to be cutting edge in the publishing world. He was absolutely blown away and suggested I reach out to him. It combined hybrid publishing with crowd funding and allowed for unrestricted creativity. My gut exploded with reinforcement that this was finally my publishing avenue. It also meant that Hank would be handling all my printing, as he was their sole printer.

When I contacted Ray, the founder, he explained that he was doing a soft launch and had a global plan in place, which included Oprah's network. He was getting success stories together before then, and I knew I had to be one of them. The issue, of course, was that I wasn't myself. I was hardly able to function, and the force trying to stop me was at an all-time high. However, there was no way I was giving up.

61

FREE AT LAST

It all happened so fast. I had caught the manuscript up and put it to the side. Something urged me to check online for apartment listings, and the first place I looked at called to me. I e-mailed the owner, and we made plans to meet in the morning.

I was greeted by a joyful man named Wayne. He was seventy-five, bald, and filled with youthful energy. I loved him immediately. *Ha, how clever—Wayne!*

However, when I looked at the studio, it was obvious that it wasn't right for me, but there was an overpowering feeling that I was supposed to live in that building. I told him that I wanted him to be my landlord but that I needed more space.

He quickly informed me that there was a unit downstairs available, and when I walked in, my guides loudly informed me that I had finally found my home. The place needed a lot of work but had so much character. Without me even asking, he lowered the rent for me, and we signed the paperwork.

Almost immediately I began moving in, but it wasn't until I actually shut the door and locked it behind me that it hit me. I still don't know why it didn't click sooner. This was the white house with black shutters in the exact city that Dawn had predicted. My jaw just dropped. *Wow, I made it.*

Something radical shifted within. It was as though my light went a thousand times brighter. This meant that the guy who was predicted was right around the corner. Then it happened. A blinding, stabbing pain blasted into my lower back and repeated over and over. I started gasping for air but couldn't breathe.

I collapsed in pain for the first time in my life and actually thought I was dying. Then *something* left my body, and I felt more like me than I had in years.

It was such a relief, but then the horror and damage of the nightmare came more into focus. *How did that get so out of control? What happened these last few years? How can there be such a path of destruction? How humiliating. How painful.*

I shook my head as I analyzed how hard I had hit rock bottom, how dark my dark night of the soul had been, and how much my life had been damaged. I had no idea how to accept any of it as true. I had pushed my family and friends away to protect them, suffered a major personality shift, watched my life fall apart, and had been allowing myself to destroy every facet of my well-being because the possession had become so unbearable. I was struggling to connect emotionally with people I had known before or during the trauma. I had wanted out for so long. Life without a soul is not life.

I didn't even recognize my body anymore—it was so weakened. I did my best not to be angry about having something hellish take the reins of my life as it controlled my whole being, prancing me around in an idiotic way and doing the same to the people around me, turning loved ones into enemies. *Why did this happen? Is it so that I can raise awareness about possession since it's at an all-time high—including the United States?*

I couldn't believe that I was finally living in the part of the story that I had ached for. There was so much work ahead of me, but I had already committed to an intense four-day training session down in San Jose that my friend David had an extra ticket for because his friend couldn't go at the last minute. He thought the training would be beneficial for me and he said it was a unique opportunity.

So there I was with a massive project ahead of me, in the storyline I had ached for, in need of serious healing, and I had to leave right then and there. It was almost impossible to walk out the door. I didn't even know who was presenting. I didn't want to step away from my new reality and not see the rest of the predictions come pouring in. I didn't want it to all disappear.

I went down anyway, and my mind was blown instantly. It was Brendon Burchard, the world's highest-paid marketing advisor, and he was teaching us how to be successful in videos, marketing, and sales. The timing was epic in terms of my book and the videos I was about to start making. His energy was absolutely addictive, and the networking was top of the line.

Meanwhile, I was trying not to freak out in my body, as I had just endured a radical shift in my energy field. It was like coming out of a coma and being thrown into a party. There was also an outrageous rash that had appeared when the entity left my body, so I was feeling especially attractive. (There's a sentence you never think you'll say.)

Brendon repeatedly talked about Dr. Wayne Dyer and how they had worked together and been friends. He even said that his purpose was to carry on Wayne's legacy, and the warmest feeling flooded my body. *Exactly, everything is intention. My purpose is to teach intention too! Loud and clear, Wayne!*

He told his story about being a struggling writer, being in a horrible car accident, and even being suicidal. In that exact moment, he gave me permission to talk about my own battle with suicidal thoughts, and I set my intentions to take his advice and one day shake his hand for giving me that courage. *Wow, thank you, Brendon! Thank you, Wayne! Thank you for writing the ending of this book!*

That life-changing weekend sent me skyrocketing back to my new world. The whole ride home, I had to convince myself that I hadn't imagined it. I was rocking a new energy field, and Brendon was now permanent fuel on my fire. I was coming back to life. Dawn's predictions began to snowball even more.

62

MY TWIN FLAME

There are no words for how much I loved my new home and for how kind Wayne and his wife were. Step by step, I was struggling to rebuild and heal. However, everything was still distorted around me, as the attacks continued.

Meanwhile, with the help of my very talented friend, we put together a book campaign and worked many hours on a promotional video with some other friends. The force trying to stop Brian and me was unbearable, but we didn't give up. These were the early, awkward stages of getting comfortable in front of the camera. The dancing wasn't what it is when I'm alone by any means, but it was a start.

This was also the moment that I realized how much I love directing consciousness videos and working with a collaborative team. My purpose was coming into focus even more. *Okay, Universe, I want to direct videos that can inspire people while working with a creative team and traveling. I want to heal as many people as possible and teach through my passions, especially dance. I want to be an artistic director and write lyrics for spoken word! How do I make this happen at the level I am intending?*

I knew the answer. At this time, I started to call in my twin flame through meditation because I knew that it was time for him to enter my life. I needed him, and I was done pushing him away. He had been predicted to come in at this time, and I was finally ready. I had awareness that he was going to be a catalyst for an unrivaled transformation.

I prayed and prayed for that energy field to come blasting into my life and to just plop down in front of me. *Thank you for this being obvious! Thank you for this happening soon!* For weeks, I kept saying, "He's coming in soon; I can feel it." Wow, could I.

I kept being blasted by waves of his energy field as he was magnetized in. It was so intense that I made a vision board after not making one for a year. On this one I used an image of two puzzle pieces, one said "You" and the other said "Me" as they were fitting together. I even put it on there twice.

Miraculously, that's exactly what happened. Two weeks later he sat down right in front of me, the day after I finished the video project for the book. I knew that soul instantly. Despite the familiarity, it was as shocking as spotting a leprechaun. We quickly bonded over our love of food, music, art, nature, and spirituality. We even talked admiringly about the late Wayne Dyer.

I was shocked that I had met him in the short time period that Dawn had predicted, because she had said I would meet him in wine country within a few months of moving into the white house with black shutters. It was so specific.

He asked me out moments later as we made plans to go to a nice local restaurant. He then said, "Before we go there, we should go to Morimoto," my favorite sushi restaurant, where I won the trip to Hawaii—and right near my new home. We set a date and couldn't stop talking. I will refer to him as J-man.

A random incident forced us to reschedule, which landed our first date on the night of the strawberry moon, meaning it was the only time the full moon had coincided with the June Solstice since 1967—likely the only one in our lifetime. There was magical energy where air used to exist.

When we met there, we were dressed alike in turquoise shirts—a color that I had never worn before. It was so ridiculous. The beautiful thing about it all was that I wasn't nervous or trying to impress him. Our energy just clicked together, like it always does.

We were extremely engaged, and at one point I looked under the table to see his feet because that is the part of the body that tell us the most about how we are feeling; it's the limbic system revealing the truth. His legs were completely stretched toward me under the table, and his feet were bouncing around with excitement as if they were reaching for me. My smile spread wider.

Neither of us got up even once that whole drawn-out dinner. His energy was off the charts, unprecedented. He was impressively grounded with a massive heart and a smile so infectious I couldn't wipe mine away if I tried. He was also absolutely hilarious, so the laughing never stopped. We talked about our humanity mission and our shared interests. It was wild how much we had in common. We both kept commenting on the energy and how much we were enjoying the stimulating conversation.

I couldn't believe that I was sitting across from the man I have always sensed. My soul was doing cartwheels of recognition. What was extra shocking was that he filled out Dawn's predictions like marking boxes on a checklist. He directed music videos, worked with a creative team, was a singer/songwriter, was talented at painting, traveled for work with a camera crew and had a burning desire to help people. He wore dynamic very well, and our passions aligned with a surgeon's precision.

So that meant that I wanted to be with him, work for him, work on creative projects with him, and then help as many people as possible with him. It was convoluted. He was everything, and more, in one package. That was scary.

He told me he was currently writing a song about magic over lust. I refrained from telling him that I was writing a book about the magic of the universe and that he had been a predicted character in it for years. Dawn had told me to play my cards tight with him, but it was so hard to keep it all in. It didn't take much to be completely swept off my feet. I never stood a chance.

When we hugged good-bye, there was a dramatic zap of energy. As I floated home, I heard, *"You won't hear from him for a couple of weeks."* It made me sad, but J-man and I had talked about the ebb and flow of energy—this was going to take a while to marinate. That was obvious.

That night when I went to bed, there were two dramatic blasts of bright, sparkling color a few feet from my face. I shook my head and thought I was losing it. Then the next morning, there were two more right when I woke up. The colors were red, blue, violet, and green. It was as though my chakras exploded. My whole energy field had shifted immensely.

As sensed, we didn't talk for a couple of weeks. I started having precognitive dreams with him in them all the time. We were frequently working on projects and traveling.

We had another amazing date, which landed on the full moon again, and he continued to impress me beyond my comprehension—his linguistics systematically seducing me.

Another night he came over for dinner at my place, and I've never seen anyone get so excited about food. He kept saying that he could envision my TV show and started talking about how he could help. Our energetic connection had amplified. I just wanted to melt into him but again left it at a hug and didn't tell him he was a main character in my book and the answer to my prayers.

After that, he started to do more of what twin flames do: run. As much as I knew I wanted to be with him, there was a part of me running too. With twin flames, there is generally a runner and a chaser, but I just didn't have it in me to chase. It's also about deeply working on yourself, and it's really overwhelming to reconnect such intense energy. The level of required vulnerability was terrifying, to say the least. I also didn't want to mess it up.

He continued giving me advice on the book and offered to connect me with the right people, but we weren't hanging out. We continued our inside joke on the nights of the full moon and would randomly catch up on our lives.

Even on the phone, I would get zapped with outrageous energy. I ached for him to stop running—especially since he had my heart with him. However, I also knew the timing would work out divinely and that I needed to be focusing on myself. I was going through a wild transformation.

63

WELCOME TO DREAMLAND

Ms. Erika came up to visit me, and I was finally able to open up about the possession more, and she insisted that I reach out to a specific multidimensional healer who helps people who have experienced that type of trauma.

During the reading, she told me that J-man and I would definitely end up working on a project together, just like my recurring dreams, and that we would take things very slowly. She commented on how many similarities we had and said that he wasn't ready for me yet—and he didn't want to mess it up.

She reminded me that twin flames have a lot of internal work to do, and it can be really overwhelming. She also told me not to tell him the twin flame part yet. Either way, it gave me the peace of mind that I needed.

She continued to provide more clarity and healing than I had even anticipated. She told me that I was moving soon and named the exact area that I had fallen in love with on my drive up to Northern California—Zen Island. She told me that I was going to finish the book there and get into holistic energy medicine. She predicted that I would be taking classes, creating podcasts, selling products, doing spoken word, promoting my artwork, and getting my messages out in creative ways to market the book.

She even predicted that I was going to win a lot of money, just like Dawn had said. It was the pot of gold at the end of the rainbow. The magnetic pull was stronger than any other move. I had been pulled there aggressively recently, and now it was officially time to make the jump. She had realigned me and provided so much clarity about certain people in the book.

She told me that Antix and I parallel each other and that I would end up working with Ricky Williams. She told me to reach out to the former radio show host, to Neil Strauss and to his sound guy, Scott. Everything she said resonated and was what I had been instinctually feeling.

However, soon afterwards, the PTSD started to trigger several times due to the transition, and I was fading in and out. The sensation was equivalent to the undertow in the ocean, dragging me out to sea. I couldn't think straight.

In a matter of weeks though, I jumped to the coastal beach area she had predicted and felt home at last in Zen Island. For the first time, I was able to stop the PTSD trajectory and regain some control. This time, I decided that it wasn't going to stop me anymore, especially during times of stress. I just refused to lose any more of my life.

I was undergoing a radical metamorphosis. I was breaking out of a cocoon and spreading my wings. I wasn't chasing anymore, and I wasn't being chased. The tornado finally spit me out, and

I was free.

Immediately I was magnetized to Lee Holden, an internationally known Qi Gong master. Wayne kept pushing me toward his classes; there was clearly something he needed to teach me.

Lee is an amazing teacher and an obvious inspiration. I eventually figured out that he had been friends with Wayne Dyer—of course. His classes changed my life and transformed my mind and body.

I needed that form of healing my entire life and I became personally dedicated to sending as many people as possible toward this practice so they can feel as alive and healed as I do. Lee's online videos have helped so many people in my life. Our solution is life-force energy—it heals and unites us.

Then, just like that, I was living in the final predictions. Instantly I began working in the field of holistic energy medicine, taking classes, revving my artistic expression, wrapping up the book, and meeting more of my people. I moved into a beach house, in an area surrounded by the redwoods—and I play in nature constantly.

I found my spiritual tribe of healers and finally understood my true purpose. It was the land of abundance. I had found the pot of gold I had been searching for my whole life.

The reunion with my whole soul allowed me to find my peace, and everything clicked into its destined place. I finally understood my gift, and I was no longer scared of it. I was just completely dedicated to using it to help others. It was the Chicago experience with a drastically happier ending—a truly happy ending—because I found my peace within. I found my freedom.

I became healthier, more focused, and more alive than ever. I became happier than I ever thought possible. My hunger for life and global change is uncontainable—people are constantly commenting on my energy. I'm so grateful the nightmare is over. I'm also grateful for the nightmare. I never thought I would say that.

The light at the end of the tunnel was brighter than I had thought possible. I am constantly surrounded by healers, philanthropists, revolutionary thinkers, artists, light workers, thought leaders, superheroes of change, ancient souls, entertainers and those who are awake.

We are dedicated to making as much of a difference as we possibly can. It's time to show the world how practical peace really is. It's time for a solution-focused, healing revolution—with lots of dancing. The only way to conquer the dark is to turn up the light. If my darkness can morph into a plane of illumination—then anything is possible.

Let's unite like never before and raise our collective vibrations. Let's show this world what we are made of! It starts with you and your inner healing!

We are at a turning point, and we have two options. We can keep doing what we have been conditioned to do or make a 180-degree shift. We can choose soul over ego. We can choose love over fear. We can have faith in the source. We can expect miracles. We can free ourselves.

It's like that scene in the movie *Finding Nemo* where all the fish are being captured, and they are panicking and working against each other. However, when they start swimming together in the same direction, they are released. Our choice is to continue being divided and conquered or to unite and prosper. How brilliant that we actually have a choice. What will we choose?

With that said, I must say goodbye to my sweet sociopath. Goodbye, demons. Goodbye, suffering. Goodbye, fear.

Goodbye, tornado. Goodbye, nightmare to reach my dreams. I can't say I will miss you—at all—but thank you for serving your purpose. I'm so grateful for you!

I'm so curious to see what happens next! If you want to see, please find me at www.dreamboldnetwork.com. The rest is history!

About the Author

MS. K is absolutely obsessed with Law of Attraction, miracles and this world's potential. With a background in human services, non-profit and personal development, she believes that humanity can work together and achieve absolutely anything!

She has a Masters degree in Psychology and is a certified life coach and NLP practitioner—but it's her fiery passion, wild imagination, mistakes and faith in the power of the Universe that are the foundation of her credentials. She is adventurous, polarized, un-definable and absolutely silly. She doesn't fit in the box—and she questions everything!

She has a huge heart and truly believes that humanity has a brighter, more abundant and more magical future than we are being conditioned to believe. She is dedicated to proving this and to making philanthropy more exciting and creative than ever.

MS. K is crazy enough to think that we can change the world—and she intends to show humanity how to create miracles so that the people can manifest that change and find our peace!

STAY CONNECTED WITH MS. K
For more of MS. K's work, please visit:
Dreamboldnetwork.com

Bonus Thoughts

The simplest way that I can think of to explain the art of manifesting is to envision it like going to a restaurant. You have a menu of options, you decide what you want, you visualize yourself having what you want, you experience the emotions of it before it happens, you have complete faith that it will show up, you are grateful that you're about to experience it, you detach from it while still expecting it to show up, and then you exist in a state of receiving. So what do you want to order?

Of course, it's more complex than that and there are many techniques that help you manifest your desires. The reality is that it's always working for each and every one of us and it's just a matter of whether or not we harness this innate ability to create our desires. It's a commitment, and completely worth it to tune into your super powers!

The greatest thinkers, scholars, philosophers and teachers were in agreement about the power of intention, and when we honor ancient truth and wisdom we become unstoppable. Our thoughts create our reality and the awareness of our thoughts allows us to create any life we dare to dream up! So dream bold!

I am often asked how I manifest so quickly, easily and profoundly. The answer for me is that I am obsessed with the

Law of Attraction and I intentionally use it every single day. My faith in the process is unshakeable because the more I believe in it and the more I expect miracles—well, the more they show up! It's a Universal law for a reason! It is the most fun, mind-blowing and entertaining thing I have ever experienced. It is my entire life and my greatest passion! I believe it's our solution to absolutely everything!

I would like to reiterate the importance of allowing your imagination to run wild with zero limitations. This is key in this process. The expectation of your manifestations and the patience required to allow them to show up in your life are necessary as well. Adding intense emotion to your thoughts speeds this process up and gratitude is the fuel that revs this fire of creation. This is quantum physics, so pay attention to your inner vibration—that's the magnet pulling in what you see around you. Your thoughts create the energy of that magnet, and you are the controller of your thoughts. How cool is that!

Masters of the Law of Attraction are in a similar state to children in that they daydream about what they desire, there are no restrictions, there is absolute faith, they are excited for their future, and they are playful in the process. Children are tapped into the source, and when you reconnect with the source in that same way, the magic shows up! Are you curious what you can create? Do you want to feel the joy you felt as a child? What would happen if you expected miracles? Make it happen!

Let's get real—this is not a process that can be learned overnight. It takes a lot of work to rewire your thinking, but it's beyond worth it to master your mind so that you are in the vibration of abundance. Just keep studying, never ever give up, and have fun tweaking your techniques! Imagine what your life could look like! How hungry are you?

Personal Recommendations

I love Hay House books—enjoy finding teachers that resonate with you!

SOME OF MY FAVORITE AUTHORS

Wayne Dyer

Mike Dooley

Bob Proctor

Esther and Jerry Hicks

Jack Canfield

Gabby Bernstein

Deepak Chopra

Boni Lonnsburry

Joseph Murphy

Doreen Virtue

Catherine Ryan Hyde

Louise Hay

Eckhart Tolle

THE RULE BREAKER

Seth Godin

Lynda Madden Dahl

Julia Rogers Hamrick

Tim Ferris

Brene Brown

Bob Doyle

Jeanette Maw

Laura Silva

Gregg Braden

Alan Watts

NETFLIX SUGGESTIONS
The Secret
What the bleep do we know?
Happy (documentary)

DEFINITELY CHECK OUT
Brendon Burchard

Lee Holden

Neil Strauss

Mindvalley Academy

Conscious rappers

www.wakeup-world.com

THE ADVENTURE CONTINUES AT
Dreamboldnetwork.com